Military Bands

MILITARY BANDS

and their uniforms

Jack Cassin-Scott & John Fabb

BLANDFORD PRESS   POOLE   DORSET

© Jack Cassin-Scott and John Fabb
First published 1978 in Great Britain
by Blandford Press Ltd,
Link House, West Street, Poole, Dorset

ISBN 0 7137 0895 6

Printed in Great Britain
by the Hope Burgess Group, London and Abingdon,
on 115 gsm Blade Coated Cartridge

There are several inaccuracies in this book. I have amended and. JMS Feb 1984

CONTENTS

Front and reverse of London Irish Rifles Pipe-banner presented to them by the Duke of Connaught

Seliakus 1st Regiment Drum Major

French Drummer of the horse grenadiers

INTRODUCTION Instruments of the Band

Military music has always been a stirring sound. The tramp of marching feet, the steady ranks of glistening brass, the beat and rattle of the drums, still attract people and hold them spellbound.

Military music is international – a British march may also be a popular German tune, while the style of performance goes back to the old Turkish Empire. The best military music knows no frontiers.

In the earliest period of organised military bands the musicians were often civilians, hired and paid for by the officers of the regiment. Poorer regiments disbanded their musicians when not required, and the players returned to their normal occupations. But the British Royal Artillery had an organised band since 1763 which accompanied the Regiment on active service.

In action on the battlefield, the regimental band played lively airs and patriotic music to inspire the soldiers. The bandsmen were not armed, except for token swords purely for show on ceremonial occasions, and their occupation was therefore a dangerous one. In early times drummers and fifers were not officially part of the band, but fought in the ranks with the other men.

Orders in the field were transmitted by the trumpeters, and the trumpet became the most important instrument of the band, often decorated with banners bearing the regimental or the royal crest. Such badges became costly regimental items.

Kettledrums, used by the cavalry, were also decorated with banners

Early nineteenth century engraving showing a French musician using his bassoon to hold back a Russian soldier

Trumpet Banner of the Bombay Body Guard

Trumpet Banner of the Maharaja of Rambur's Regiment

A Kettle Drum of the 2nd Battalion, The Royal Ulster Rifles

similarly emblazoned. The drums themselves were often made of solid silver – such as those of the British Household Cavalry.

Military bands in the French service reached a zenith of perfection and magnificence during the First Empire. The drum horses of the cavalry regiments were richly caparisoned, especially those of the Imperial Guard. *The Grenadiers à cheval de la Garde* used a heavily embroidered

French Bandsmen. Engravings of a negro cymbalist and a horn player 1800–1810, after paintings by Hoffman

shabraque on their mounts decorated with eagles, grenades and wreaths. The drum banners were treated in the same way and the harness was richly decorated, even to the point of a feather headdress for the horse.

During the revolutionary period in France military music became extremely popular at all kinds of public functions and festivities. Under Napoleon the bands of the infantry regiments were stabilised into some-

opposite: *French Napoleonic Band. Foot grenadiers of the 1st Regiment Imperial Army Old Guard 1804–1815. 'Pioneers; drum major, lead drummer; drummers; fifers; musicians; Colonel and Lieut. Colonel'*

Sapeurs (1)   Tambour-Major (2) Caporal-Tambour (3)   Tambours (4)

Tambours   Fifres (5)

Musiciens (6)

Musiciens   Musicien-Maître

Musiciens   Colonel général commandant les grenadiers   Colonel général en second

French horn   *Cor de chasse*

thing resembling the modern military band. They had about sixteen clarinets and four bassoons, with a high clarinet and a piccolo for the highest registers and two serpents for the lowest. In the brass, there were two trumpets and a bass trumpet, four horns and three trombones. The percussion consisted of a bass drum and two side drums, with two pairs of cymbals, two turkish crescents and a triangle.

The most ancient European brass instrument is the horn, originally the hunting horn of medieval times. The French in the seventeenth century produced a slender hunting horn with a wide bell which had a much extended range of harmonics and a loud brilliant tone. The French horn was more popular in Europe than in Britain – it was adopted for his own military bands by Frederick the Great of Prussia, himself a talented musician. Detachable crooks were used to extend the harmonic range. The French horn was (and is) a difficult instrument to play, and horn players in early military bands were paid a higher wage than the other musicians. The modern valved instrument is versatile; it can produce a smooth mellow tone or a strident blast.

The trumpet is perhaps the best known military band instrument after the drums. It had been the custom for a king's herald to be accompanied by trumpets since the Middle Ages. The herald was a most important personage, but the trumpeters were also men of standing. This trumpet was long and without any valves, the sound controlled by the mouth of the musician. The cavalry trumpet was coiled to make it easier to manage on horseback, and was used to control the movement of regiments and to pass on messages or signals to other regiments. One of the most famous calls is from the Italian cavalry '*Buite Sella*', which translated means 'mount on saddles', usually interpreted as 'boots and saddles'.

The French had evolved signals by use of trumpets in the early sixteenth century, a list of these was published by Mersenne in 1635. The trumpeters

Boot and Saddle

who accompanied the heralds were dressed in costly uniforms. This tradition followed in the cavalry regiments, the trumpeters always wearing costly and brilliant uniforms. The trombone appeared in military bands at the beginning of the nineteenth century, but had an earlier history dating back to the fourteenth century in northern Italy. It was introduced to British military bands by the Germans who had used it widely since the eighteenth century. The bass or tuba, as it was sometimes called, was widely used by the German and French military bands of the early nineteenth century, and later by the British and Americans.

The tenor horn or saxhorn was and still is very popular in European military bands and is related to the bass, being of course much smaller and easier to handle. The original instrument, called a serpent, was made of wood and was cumbersome to carry, especially by the military. A Frenchman invented a new instrument called the upright serpent, which was much easier to carry, indeed the mouth was made in the shape of a serpent with the mouth open and usually of brass. From this evolved the other types of bass.

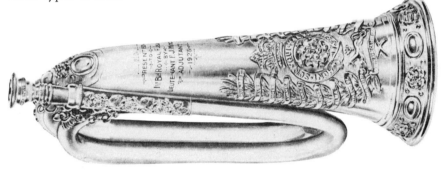

Bugle   The Royal Fusiliers   1923
This silver bugle has raised designs at the mouthpiece and at the bell, consisting of the regimental crest and battle honours of the 1st Battalion The Royal Fusiliers (City of London Regiment). This is a presentation bugle by one of the regimental officers.

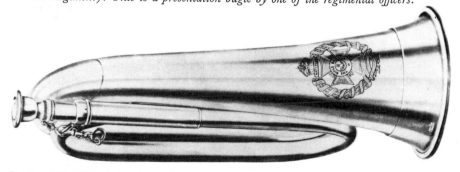

Bugle   The Rifle Brigade   c.1929
This bugle was made in white metal. Steelspun and planished, and engraved with the regimental crest, this cost 4 gns and with the addition of battle honours engraved would cost extra.

The fife is another very ancient instrument used by the Greeks in the Heriic Period. The Swiss mercenaries of the Middle Ages used them, accompanied by the drums. This combination was used by many armies and was to be found in the British service again in the early eighteenth century after going out of fashion at the end of the English Civil War.

The bugle which is the companion of the trumpet is an essential military band instrument and like the trumpet has a variety of uses, especially that of giving signals such as 'To Arms' or 'The Last Post'. The word bugle is old French and translated means young bull. It was used in hunting. The Germans and British adopted it for military uses and it was copied for the Russian army about the period of Waterloo, also at this time many more keys were added and it became a more versatile instrument.

The bag-pipe which is one of the most difficult instruments to master, has a number of variations in Europe. In Ancient Egypt a similar instrument was used. The Romans introduced it to the British Isles and to Ireland where they have been used since the fifteenth century. The old German 'dudelsack' had separate chanters on which two-part melodies could be played. In Scotland the pipes were held in special esteem within the clans and, with the formation of Highland regiments, pipes were included as a matter of course. The pipers were soldiers as well as musicians and always accompanied Highland regiments into battle, even to the present day. Many pipers have won awards for gallantry for building

Bagpipes
This bagpipe is complete with the banner that depicts the donor's crest, in this case, Arthur, Duke of Connaught, a younger son of Queen Victoria. It is made from specially seasoned African black wood, fully mounted in silver, complete with cords and tassels. Sometimes the mountings were of ivory.

morale and leading the men into the thick of battle. Due to the influence of Scottish troops stationed in India, pipe bands are numerous within the armies of Pakistan and India, even a mounted pipe band was formed.

The reed instruments used in military bands come from Spain and southern France. The oboe was used by the Germans and considered suitable for military bands and was much the same as the French instrument called a French hoboy, and was introduced to the British by Charles II on his return from exile in France.

The bassoon, because of its shape called a horse's peg, has been popular in European military bands since the eighteenth century. In the nineteenth century the Belgian, Adolphe Saxe, invented the saxophone. Of the nine different types in military music, the alto and tenor were the most popular. The clarinet, made popular by Frederick the Great at about the middle of the eighteenth century, was first invented in Saxony in the late seventeenth century.

The cymbals came from Turkey and spread across Europe from Poland after the king of Poland had been presented with a Turkish band in 1700. Also at this time a long staff decorated with a crescent and numerous bells and tassels came into being. This was nicknamed 'Jingling Johnnie' by the British and was an immediate success in the French, Italian and British armies. They have survived the longest in the German armies and became most elaborate and magnificent in the period before the last war.

In America the military music had been introduced by the British and developed in much the same manner. The U.S. Navy were especially noted for playing patriotic military music and became famous at the end of the last century under the baton of Philip Sousa, America's most idolised military composer. In Europe also bandmasters became household names, Starke in Austria, Hutschenruyer in Holland and Weiprecht in Prussia.

Band schools were established, in Berlin the Hoch Schule für Musik opened a section for military bands. The Royal School of Kneller Hall was founded in 1857, and in 1888 the U.S. Military Academy created a section for the teaching of military music.

Although the craft of soldiering has lost its appeal to many of the world's population, a military band has not. The music of a brass band has always

Trumpet 1903
This trumpet was made in sterling silver and supplied by Potters and Co. for the Imperial Heralds for the Proclamation in India at the Delhi Durbar in January 1903 for the Coronation of Edward VII.

attracted the populace, indeed to cement good relations, the army always use a good military band. Tours and shows are arranged and at military tattoos one may see musicians from all parts of the world proving that music, especially military music, has an appeal that knows no political, military or musical boundaries.

BASS HORN c. 1826

At the time of the French Revolution a refugee in England named Frichot invented the bass horn, based on the upright serpent (illustrated elsewhere). The instrument did not replace the serpent, but was used in conjunction with it. Soon after the Napoleonic Wars bass horns were in common use by all military bands. But the serpent outlived the bass horn, also called the English bass horn.

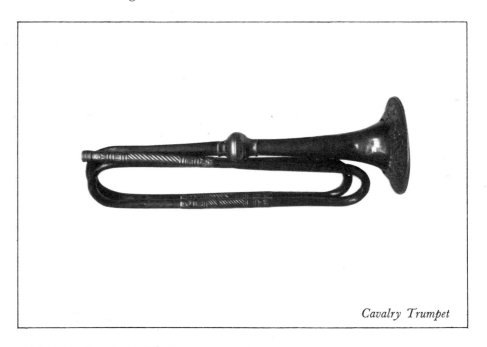

Cavalry Trumpet

CAVALRY TRUMPET

This is a natural trumpet, having no mechanical devices or valves, and it is coiled twice to make its length possible to handle on horseback. It is used as a signalling instrument and passes the commands of the colonel to the regiment who, in the din of battle, cannot hear the word of command, German army trumpeters used to play a short introduction to warn the men that a call of command was about to be given. No other armies, apparently, adopted this interesting innovation.

CLARINET c. 1800

This is a single reed instrument with cylindrical bore ending in a small bell. It gives a higher tone than a trumpet. The clarion is its third register of notes and has a wide range of over three octaves, which is divided into four registers, the lowest being called chalumeau.

Military bands contain as many as twenty-five clarinets, usually the B flat instrument and the E flat for the highest range.

*Clarinet and
Pastoral Oboe*

CLARINET AND PASTORAL OBOE

Clarinets were adopted by military bands in the mid-eighteenth century. The clarinet is a single reed instrument with a cylindrical bore forming into a small bell. It is an important and leading instrument in military bands. There are usually two E flat clarinets in a band, two in B flat and up to ten an octave higher. The instrument dates back from the seventeenth century – thought to have been invented by Denner of Nuremberg as a substitute for the ancient bass clarinet.

The oboe is an ancient military band instrument and has been long connected with processional music. It was in its earlier form a hautbois or hoboy and even before that, the waite pipe. There are usually up to thirty oboes in a military band.

The eighteenth century oboe with two keys was already in use by German military bands. In Britain it was introduced to the Horse Grenadiers in 1678. As it had been brought from France (by the exiled Charles II in 1660) it was then called a French holboys.

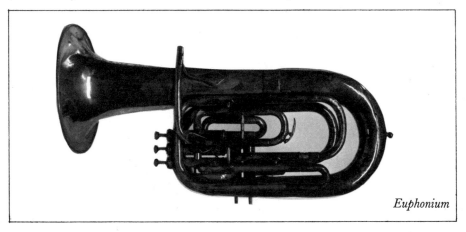

Euphonium

EUPHONIUM

This is a powerful instrument and is the bass of military bands. It can sound as many as five octaves. In addition to the normal three valves it may have a fourth valve which extends the range of notes downwards.

The euphonium evolved from the tenor horn. In Germany it is known as the *baryton*. In Britain the name baritone is given to the tenor saxhorn. The euphonium is a tenor tuba in B flat. Larger, deeper sounding tubas are in E flat and B flat; known as bombardons, or EE flat and BB flat basses. Those with circular forms to go round the body of a marching bandsman are called helicons.

FRENCH HORN

This is a very powerful instrument and in a band of thirty, only two French horns are necessary. Its carrying power is due to the conical mouthpiece and long, gradually expanding tube which flares into a wide bell at the end. It can sound sixteen or more harmonic notes, and with valves this can be increased considerably.

It is a very difficult instrument to play and a player requires a good ear to become accomplished.

The French horn was introduced to military bands in the eighteenth century and only later adopted into the symphony orchestra.

HUNTING HORN

The long, coiled *cor de chasse,* or hunting horn, was used in the various bands of the French King, Louis XIV. Hunting and equestrian interests were an important feature of court life. The bands had the title: *La grande Ecurie du Roi.*

The instrument was not popular in England, having been introduced at the restoration of Charles II. It was however used in some private bands. This instrument is made of brass and has two coils.

Coiled hunting horns originated in England in the middle ages, and spread all over Europe. Re-introduced to England as a band instrument at the restoration of Charles II, they did not become popular, but were used in some private bands. This instrument is made of brass and has two coils.

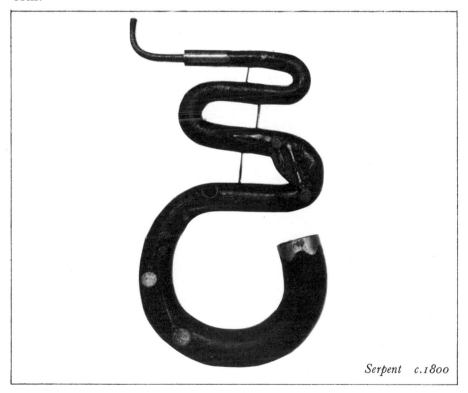

Serpent c.1800

SERPENT c. 1800

The serpent was invented by a canon of the French church at the end of the sixteenth century for use in religious music. It was popular in France and Britain and lasted until the early nineteenth century. It was a difficult instrument to manage and awkward to hold, and because of this could be easily broken.

The serpent was made of wood bound in leather. It had a conical bore and a cupped mouthpiece on a crook. It was difficult to play because of the widely spaced notes; even with keys it was not easy. Because of this an upright serpent was invented, very popular with bands in the 1820's. The mouth of the instrument was painted like a serpent, blood red with white teeth and inside a red wagging tongue which wavered as the bandsmen marched.

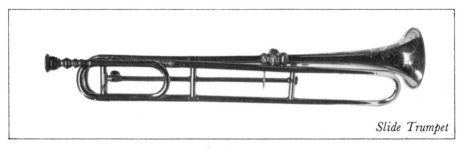

Slide Trumpet

SLIDE TRUMPET

In the late eighteenth century the British trumpeter, John Hyde, designed a slide trumpet of this type. A 'U' shaped slide took the place of the bend nearest the player and could be easily moved while playing; it was returned by a spring.

The slide trumpet was gradually replaced by the valved trumpet at the end of the nineteenth century. It was difficult to play and, being affected by temperature changes, needed very careful tuning.

VALVE BUGLE

In 1810 an Irish bandmaster named Joseph Halliday put six key holes in an army bugle and so extended its scale considerably. This instrument was called a key bugle. In Europe the Frenchman, Halari, made one in the lowest key, called an ophicleide. Keyed bugles were the only instrument playing chromatically other than the trombone until replaced by the valved instruments. The valved bugle is in fact the *Flugelhorn*, deriving from Austria.

German Drum and Fife,
17th century

DRUM AND FIFE

The fife instrument has always been associated with the carrying drums; the German name still being 'trommel-flote' (drum flute). The side drum carried then was wider and deeper than the modern drum of today, the sound was duller and lacked the crisp note of its modern counterpart. The drum is possibly the oldest of all military musical instruments and its association with warfare covers many centuries. It was first introduced into Europe during the Crusades. The military kettledrums were taken from the mounted bands of the Turkish army in the fifteenth century, the medieval Islamic name being 'nakers'. These were somewhat smaller than those in present use.

The drum and fifes were the earliest and the most basic of military music, although previously used to keep the troops in step and help keep them on the move, drummers and fifers had special duties within the army.

Bass Drum and Side Drums
The bass drum is of the Governor General's Foot Guards of Canada with a painted design consisting of the royal arms with the regimental badge below, flanked by the battle honours. The side drums are of the 1st Grenadier Guards and the 1st Coldstream Guards, both of painted designs on a brass shell. Below the royal coat of arms can be seen the regimental badges.

The drums and fifes were used to transmit signals causing their instruments to relay messages and commands. For this latter service they were often paid out of public funds, although they were in most cases paid for and maintained by the officers of the regiment, as they were not considered as part of the band.

In England drums and fifes came in about the reign of Henry VIII following the continental military music started by King Francis I of France. During the Spanish Armada crisis, drums and fifes were in evidence in the Portsmouth encampment in 1584. The assignment of drums and fifes to each company of foot in the English army at St. Quentin was ordered in 1557. This order was revoked by James II and the custom was abolished and only the drummers were retained.

The fifes however were reinstated in 1747 by the then Commander-in-Chief of the British army, the Duke of Cumberland. The first British regiment to receive both instruments was the 19th Foot, the Green Howards. The fifer usually carried two or more fifes in a case or in his pocket, these were of various sizes and pitch. A simple six-holed fife called the 'zwerch-pfeiff' (Swiss pipe) was first played by the mercenary soldiers (mainly Swiss) who joined the services of many of the European rulers in the early part of the sixteenth century. The Vatican still retains the Swiss Guard who wear the uniform of this early period. The soldier musicians of this period were respected as being non-combatants and their lives, if captured, were more often than not spared. Both drummers and fifers had further duties within the army, that of escorting dignitaries and hostages. Opposing armies took great prestige from capturing their enemies' drums in battle.

The musicians illustrated in the plate are wearing the fashions of the beginning and the middle of the seventeenth century. During this period, very often the soldier differed from the civilian only by his large coloured baldrick which he wore slung either over his shoulder or around his waist, and usually wore the heavier sword.

In the seventeenth century, it was the custom for armies to go into winter quarters until a spring offensive could be launched. It was the practice for the soldiers to be billeted in the towns and villages, naturally the social life of these men revolved around the town. To get the men back to their billets the innkeepers had to turn off the beer taps at 10.00 p.m. This was notified to the soldiers and the innkeepers by a drummers' Tattoo. An officer, sergeant and a drummer would commence beating and the men would have to return to their billets. After a short while the officer, sergeant and drummer would set off through the towns with the drummer beating his call, while the officer and sergeant would make sure the men had left the ale houses. It is thought that the expression Tattoo is derived from the Dutch Doe Den Tap Toe, 'Turn off the taps' and dates from when the British army was fighting in the Low Countries.

The Drummers' room of the Grenadier Guards   1899
The drummers of every batallion, though attached to one or other of the companies for the purposes of pay, lived and ate together on their own in a separate room.
From the photograph they appear to be practising. All except two are wearing the white drill shell jacket.

Drummer Bombay Pioneers c.1928
Bombay had five battalions of Pioneers.
These were disbanded in February
1933. The full dress uniform was
scarlet with white facings. This drum-
mer is wearing the khaki uniform. The
brass buttons are ornamented with
crossed axes as depicted on the drum.

3rd Gurkha Rifles   side drum   c.1936
This side drum of the 2nd Battalion of the 3rd
Queen Alexandra's Own Gurkha Rifles has an
aluminium shell for service in India with water-
proof vellum heads. It is tightened by plated rods
and brackets. The hoops are of ash and the crest
is hand painted.

Another ceremony connected with the corps of drums was the playing of 'The Rogues March' at the drumming out ceremony. Up to the middle of the nineteenth century, when a soldier was discharged with ignominy he was 'drummed out', that is, the regiment was formed up in two ranks facing inwards, one end touching the barrack gates. At the other end, the soldier and his escort were standing with the adjutant, who read out the offence and sentence. The provost sergeant then cut off his collar and cap badges, tore off the shoulder straps and his buttons and the prisoner and escort marched down the ranks while the drums and fifes played 'The Rogues March'. The sentence was repeated at intervals and when the prisoner reached the barrack gates he was ejected, the smallest drummer boy administering a kick to his posterior as the gates were shut.

Fife Case

The Royal Berkshire Regiment had a custom of officers being played into a Guest Night Dinner, once a week to a roll played on a Russian drum captured in the Crimea War of 1854/5, the drummer leading the officers into the Mess. During the First World War the officers were determined to capture a German drum so that the two could be played, this was eventually accomplished.

At the battle of Arroyo dos Molinos in 1811 during the Peninsular Campaign, the British 34th Foot Regiment captured the Band and Drum Major of the 34th French Regiment, their opposite number. These

French drums are now used by the 34th (The Border Regiment) at an annual Commemoration Ceremony.

Beating retreat is sounded on drums as well as bugles. In the seventeenth century the drummers would go on to the city walls and beat a retreat to give notice to those outside that the gates were about to be shut. This would be at sunset and the gates closed a quarter of an hour later. It later also required that no soldier would fire his musket unless he be a sentry and challenged; retreat was then also called 'Setting the Watch'.

Kettle Drum Banner
This is one of a pair of kettle drum banners made for the 19th Queen Alexandra's Own Royal Hussars. They are embroidered in gold and silver wire on white cloth and depict the monogram of Queen Alexandra. The elephant dates from the old 19th Light Dragoons who served in India. The present regiment was raised in 1860 and amalgamated in 1922 with the 15th, the King's Hussars.

Drum Major
King's African Rifles   c.1955
This drum major is from the 5th
Battalion the King's African Rifles.
The headdress is made from monkey
skins. The drum major's sash is
heavily embroidered in silver wire,
edged in silver lace. The background
to the sash is rifle green. The cords
and tassels are also rifle green.

DRUM MAJOR

In England the first mentioned drum major was the one in the reign of Charles I when he held the rank of a staff officer. The French instituted a rank of colonel-drummer, the British counteracted with the rank of drum major general in 1685. Although the dress of the band was costly, that of the drum major was a cumulation of the tailor's art, a profusion of gold lace, tassels and feathers, paid for out of the officers' pockets. The ideal person for this role was a tall, distinguished-looking soldier. The French found an ideal man in Senot, the Drum Major of the French Imperial Foot Guards. (A model in uniform is shown on page 10.) He was, in 1798, Drum Major to the Guard of the Consuls, and always carried a silver mounted mace in front of an impressive seventy-two drummers.

Drum Major and goat   1st Battalion The Welsh Regiment   1894
Sergeant Drummer McKelvey had seen fourteen years service when this photograph was taken and had joined at the age of eighteen. The goat depicted was a new recruit, his predecessor having dropped dead after a march through Wales in the previous year. The goat can also be seen on the top of the drum major's staff, the head of which, including the goat, is made of silver.

At the battle of Leipzig, in 1813, in which he had been wounded, he was holding the rank of lieutenant and as such, was retired on half-pay in 1814, but returned to the Emperor for the last battle at Waterloo, having seen service with the band throughout the whole of Napoleon's career as Emperor.

Drum Major   The London Scottish   1897
Drum Major Goodman was a very large and imposing figure, well able to give that post great dignity and bearing.
This regiment was formed in 1859 and is dressed in elcho grey. They also wore the glengarry and not the Highland feather bonnet which is usually associated with Highland regiments.
The drum major is wearing review order elcho grey uniform with blue collar and cuffs and a grey goatskin sporran.
In 1884 a volunteer band was formed with thirty members, but in 1893 this ceased to exist and a professional band replaced them, consisting of a bandmaster and thirty two bandsmen.
Colonel Robert Whyte states that "I distinctly remember on one occasion marching to Hyde Park, past Buckingham Palace, seeing the Bandmaster stumbling along quite evidently a bit worse for drink; and that was the last time they paraded with us."

Such flamboyant characters are to be found in other countries. In Great Britain the drum major of the Essex Regiment would toss his baton in the air as the band marched through the archway of the barracks, and catch it as they marched out the other side. Such gymnastics are not for Her Majesty's Guards whose majestic progress across a parade ground is a sight that cannot be described, but one that should be savoured by all militarists.

1815   Royal Artillery Band

ROYAL ARTILLERY BAND 1815
DRUMMER AND DRUM MAJOR, MUSICIANS AND NEGRO BANDSMAN

At the end of the Napoleonic Wars the bands of the allies played frequently in Paris. The Royal Artillery band at this time numbered thirty-eight. It was here that the newly invented keyed bugle used by the Coldstream Guards attracted the attention of Grand Duke Constantine of Russia, who later introduced it into the Russian army.

The Royal Artillery band at this period was dressed in white uniforms. The shako was the Belgic or Wellington shako introduced in 1811. Made of black felt with a false front higher than the crown, it was bound in black braid and had a black laquered peak. On the left side was a black silk rosette, behind this was the plume of red cut feathers. The cords were plaited white with tassels on the right side. The brass badge depicted a garter inscribed 'Royal Regiment of Artillery'. Within the garter was the royal monogram. Above the badge was a crown and below, the artillery cannon.

The white coatee was worn by the band. The blue collar was laced all round in yellow. The coatee was single-breasted and fastened by brass buttons with loops of bastion-ended yellow lace. The turnbacks were white, edged in yellow lace. They were also decorated with slashed pockets edged in a yellow lace and ornamented with brass buttons. The centre vent of the coatee was bound with yellow lace also. The rounded cuffs were of blue cloth with brass buttons and yellow bastion-ended lace decorations.

The breeches were white and fitted into black, buttoned gaiters with black shoes. For gala occasions white gaiters would have been used.

The French horn was bound with red and gold cords.

The negro bandsman, a popular member of military bands at this period, was dressed in a red cap with a white turban from which issued a red feather plume. His coatee was the same pattern as the other bandsmen's. In place of white breeches and gaiters, he wore tight-fitting red pantaloons with yellow leather pointed boots decorated with a white tassel at the front. Over the right shoulder passed a white leather belt to support the 'schellenbaum', or 'jingling johnnie' as it was more popularly called in the British army. The pattern shown differs from normal by having the large bell at the head with the crescent below. Other patterns existed with the bell below the crescent as can be seen in the illustration of the Prussian 13th Infantry of 1835 *(p.94)*.

The drum major wore a cocked hat laced in gold with a decoration of red feathers along the edge and a tall red plume at the top. The coatee was of scarlet cloth with blue fringes. It was heavily laced in gold at the front and on the cuffs, and the epaulettes had gold stripes and gold bullion fringes.

The Belgic shako was replaced in 1816 by the bell-topped shako, and in 1820 light blue trousers were introduced in place of the breeches.

OLDENBURG DRUM MAJOR AND DRUMMERS 1835

The Grand Duchy of Oldenburg supported a small army, modelled on the prussian pattern. The drum major wore a black felt bell-topped shako bound in black leather. The chin scales were silver and worn, as was the custom at the period, looped over the national cockade of red and blue. The shako was held to the head by means of a patent leather strap. The shako badge was a silver sunburst with a shield superimposed, bearing the arms of Oldenburg. From two hooks on each side of the shako a silver

Oldenburg Band

twisted cord passed over the front of the head-dress. On the left side was a small silver tassel; on the right two cords passed down to the tunic where they were attached to the left shoulder strap button and ended in two silver tassels and flounders.

The prussian blue coatee was double-breasted and fastened by two rows of eight silver buttons. The red collar was bound all round with silver lace which was piped red. The white shoulder straps were lined and edged in red, the wings were red with bands of silver lace, and the fringe was of silver and red. The sleeves of the coatee were ornamented with four chevrons of silver lace on a red ground, and the red cuffs were slashed and edged in silver lace and fastened with three silver buttons. The coatee turnbacks were red and fastened with a silver button. The drum major's cross belt was of white leather and supported a pair of black ebony drum sticks with silver fittings. From the waist hung a short infantry sword with a brass hilt, carried in a black leather scabbard with brass fittings. White linen trousers without gaiters were worn by the drum major. His staff had a silver head and was ornamented with silver chains ending with two silver tassels at the foot.

2nd East Yorkshire Volunteer Artillery   1889
This regiment, which had its headquarters at Hull, ranked thirty-eighth in the order
of precedence in Artillery Volunteers.
Drum Major Taylor had served 22 years in the army, eleven in the 3rd Dragoon Guards
and eleven as an instructor in the Yorkshire Hussars. The boy on the left was a clarionette
player named Sidney Charlton and the drummer on the right, Harry D. Blinkhorn. Both
had already served two years in the Regiment when this photograph was taken in 1899.
The uniform was very similar to that worn by the band of the Royal Artillery, except the
lacing on this regiment would have been silver.

The drummers wore the same shako as the drum major but with white cords and tassels in place of silver ones. The prussian blue coatee had a plain red standing collar and had white metal instead of silver buttons. The shoulder straps were white lined and edged in red and on the top were embroidered the regimental or battalion number in red silk. The wings were red and blue. On the sleeves were four chevrons of red lace decorated with a blue zig-zag pattern. The cuffs were red and had a blue slash ornamented by three white metal buttons.

The drums were carried on white leather straps and had brass shells. The hoops were light blue with a white band. The cords were white. The drummers also carried the short infantry sword from a belt over the right shoulder. The trousers were of white linen and were worn with white spats over black shoes.

DRUM MAJOR ROYAL ARTILLERY 1840

The scarlet coatee was worn at this period by the trumpeters and drummers. In 1850 blue coatees began to be issued and by 1851 all the band were clothed in blue. The light blue trousers were withdrawn in 1847. The picture shows Alexander Sutherland, drum major from 1829 to 1844.

The bearskin cap carried from the right side a scarlet feather plume over the top of the cap. The coatee was of scarlet cloth. The collar was blue, laced all round in gold. The plastron front was also blue and edged in gold lace, with gilt buttons and buttonholes edged in gold lace, the lace extending across the plastron front. The epaulettes had gold lace straps with gilt crescents and gold bullion fringes. The cuffs of blue cloth were rounded, the top edge being of gold lace, and they were ornamented with gilt buttons. Vertical decorations of lace extended from the buttons down to the edge of the cuff. Around the waist passed a crimson sash with crimson tassels hanging on the right side. Over the right shoulder was the sword belt, held at the chest with a brass belt plate. This depicted the cannon-and-crown crest of the Royal Artillery.

The sword carried had a brass hilt, the scabbard being black leather with brass mountings. The drum major's sash, worn over the left shoulder, was of blue cloth, lined with blue morocco leather. It was edged with gold lace and embroidered with the royal crown and coat of arms, the cannon of the regiment and the regimental mottoes. Below these were fitted the black ebony drum sticks with gilt mountings. The point of the sash was ornamented with a gold bullion tassel.

The trousers were of light blue cloth with two-inch gold lace stripes along the outer seams. At the thigh were embroidered gold lace austrian knots, which themselves were outlined in gold cord and russia braid.

Royal Artillery Drum Major

The drum major's staff is illustrated elsewhere, and is of wood with a gilt brass head and chains, and embellished with gold cords and tassels. In 1851 the drum major gave up the scarlet coatee for one of dark blue.

DRUM MAJOR ROYAL ARTILLERY 1860

The drum major of the Royal Artillery had lost his scarlet coatee in 1851, but more soberly dressed than previously, he still presented an imposing figure leading the regimental band.

The drum major at this date was James Lowerie who is illustrated on the following page. The bearskin is possibly the same as that worn before. The scarlet feather plume was fitted to the left side and encircled the top. The tunic was of dark blue cloth with a scarlet collar with rounded ends. It was laced all round in gold and had an extra decoration of russia braid in the

R.A. Drum Major (1860)

centre. The tunic was single-breasted and fastened by hooks and eyes. Across the breast were five bars of gold lace, edged in gold russia braid, twisted into ornamental ends. The cuffs were dark blue with two rows of gold lace edged with looped gold russia braid. On the forearm of each sleeve was an embroidered badge consisting of a trophy of musical instruments and banners. Above this was the regimental cannon with the royal crown overall. The trousers were also of dark blue with 1¾ inch gold lace stripes along the outer seams.

DRUM MAJOR AND DRUMMER 1st BATTALION GRENA-DIER GUARD c. 1870

These two group photographs were taken at Victoria Barracks, Windsor. The drum major stands to the left in both pictures and is holding a short marching cane used on less formal occasions. This had a twisted cord decoration ending with two tassels. Over his right shoulder hangs a crimson sash. The state dress uniform is only worn when the Sovereign is present. The drummer boys are wearing swords of a special pattern which was abolished in 1905, although the bandsmen still retained their special pattern swords which are of a different and more elaborate pattern. The bass drum player can be recognised by his apron, and the size of the drum should be noted, this has now been reduced considerably. The drum is secured by a leather belt and hooks around his neck.

Grenadier Guards   c. 1870

The extreme youth of the boys is of interest and is more noticeable on the indoor picture, the bearskin cap accentuating their diminutive size. The white lace of the tunic is woven with a blue fleur-de-lis, once part of the royal coat of arms. George III finally accepted that he was no longer able to justify the title of King of France.

In the outdoor photograph, in the pile of side drums can be seen one of the Russian pattern, and no doubt captured in the Crimean War. The body is of brass and has the decoration of the Russian Imperial eagle within an oval shield. One of the boys in this photograph is wearing the undress pillbox cap of dark blue with a red band and a brass grenade badge, and also the plain white drill jacket with brass buttons.

Drum Major's sash   2nd Battalion 8th Gurkha Rifles   c.1930

This sash is embroidered in gold and silver wire with the king's monogram and coat of arms with the regimental crest and battle honours below. The regiment was raised in 1835 and became the 2nd Battalion in 1907.

Drum Major's sash   5th Battalion 14th Punjab Regiment   1934

This regiment was raised in 1858 as the 44th Regiment; in 1861 it was altered to the 40th Bengal Native Infantry. In 1890 they became a Baluch Regiment, but were altered to Pathans in 1892. On the re-organisation of the Indian army in 1922 they received the above title, although the designation Pathans was not used until 1934. This drum major's sash is a variation in being of leather with silver fittings and badges.

Drum Major's sash   R.A.F.   c.1930

Embroidered drum major's sash on blue cloth edged with gold lace and made for the R.A.F. station at Cosford No. 1 (A) Wing. Embroidered with the cap badge and the crest of the Royal Air Force.

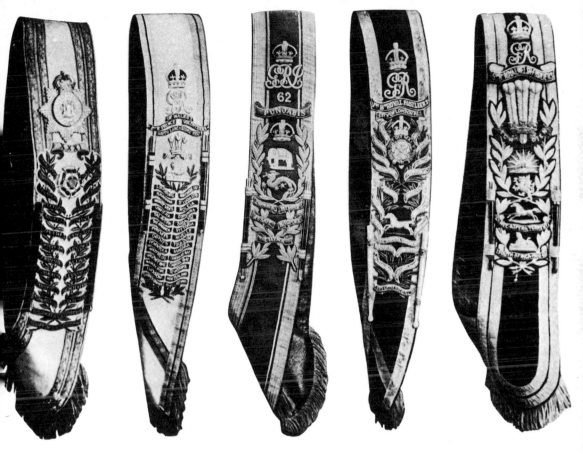

31st East Surrey Regiment

This drum major's sash is embroidered in gold and silver wire. The star badge depicts the arms of Guildford in the centre. The battle honours are embroidered on velvet scrolls.

2nd Battalion the Prince of Wales' Volunteers (The South Lancashire Regiment)

The drum major's sash has a background of pale yellow cloth, the regimental facings. All the badges and honours are embroidered in gold wire.

62nd Punjabis

This old Indian army regiment was raised in 1759 as the 2nd Madras Infantry. The tunics were scarlet with emerald green facings. The silver elephant was used as a collar badge. The drum major's sash was embroidered on a background of emerald green.

1st Battalion Royal Fusiliers City of London Regiment

The sash is embroidered on a background of blue cloth, the red rose within the gaiter being the central badge. The battle honours are interwoven with laurel leaves. The drumsticks are ivory.

5th Battalion Royal Welsh Fusiliers

This sash is one of the territorial army battalions and depicts only the South African War battle honour. The sash is embroidered in gold and silver wire. The crest of the Prince of Wales is the main badge.

Garde Nationale (1816)

TAMBOUR ET SAPEUR DE LA GARDE NATIONALE PARISIENNE 1816

It was the custom of regiments to have the sapeurs to lead the regiment with the drum major and band immediately behind. This is the reason for coupling these two figures in the illustration.

The drum major wore a hussar style busby with a loose scarlet bag ending in a silver tassel. The white ostrich and egret feather plumes issued from a silver leaf edged holder.

The coatee was of dark blue cloth, the collar white with silver lace edging. This lace had a centre line of red. The bullion epaulettes were silver as also was the frogging across the chest that ended in small silver tassels. The cuffs were white with two rows of inverted chevron silver lace above the cuff. The coatee tails were lined in scarlet. The breeches were of tight fitting white cloth and elaborately embroidered on the thighs in silver lace and silver russia braid. Silver lace also decorated the outer seams. The boots were black leather with silver laced tops and a silver tassel.

The preponderance of the white was because the colour of the House of Bourbon was white and they were the Kings of France at that time. The drum major's staff had a silver head and a silver lace binding down the shaft, similar to the pattern used on his uniform.

The drum major's sash was of red cloth lined with red morocco leather. It was edged with silver lace and a silver fringe. The decoration consisted of embroidered Bourbon lilies and a stylised pair of drumsticks. The drum major also wore a sword with a cross hilt in a plain steel scabbard with a chased shoe.

West Point and Field Music, 1872

DRUMS AND DRUM HORSES

The drums, or kettle drums, to give them their correct name, have been used by armies for several centuries, and existed in the East amongst the Mongols. They were decorated with human hair and other grisly trophies. These drums usually differed slightly in size in order that a different note could be achieved. Kettle drums were made of copper, there are exceptions when they have been made in silver. These have usually been presented by an important personage connected with the regiment concerned, or occasionally the garrison town where the regiment had been raised or stationed.

The kettle drums were used as command instruments and usually beaten in Paris. The French did not adopt the kettle drums until the reign of Louis XIV. In England Henry VIII was introduced to them by Hungarian representatives of the Holy Roman Empire, but were not adopted until the seventeeth century.

In central Europe the large kettle drums had been hauled around by an ornate carriage, usually attached to the artillery, and were especially favoured by the artillery of Frederick the Great. These drums gradually fell out of favour and were replaced by the smaller kettle drums carried on a heavy horse, often a magnificent animal, costly and of perfect breeding, a suitable companion to the drums that were the pride of the regiment. The drum banners that were hung at the front of the drums displayed the crest of the regiment of the ruler's coat of arms. These were costly items, heavily embroidered in gold and silver wire on velvet cloth. In the British and Indian army, the battle honours were also included on the banners, but on the continent of Europe this was a practice that was not followed.

DRUM AND DRUM HORSES

The drum horse reached their zenith of exotic uniform during the Napoleonic Wars. The French were particularly fond of the drum horse and its rider to show the panache and swagger of the cavalrymen.

The Mamelukes of the Imperial Guard employed a negro kettle drummer dressed in a white turban with tall white ostrich feathers, blue and white striped tunic with a red waistcoat and white pantaloons. The drum banners were of rich green velvet, edged with gold lace and fringe. They were embroidered in the centre with the Imperial eagle and the regimental title on a scroll.

The kettle drummer of the Carabiniers was dressed in powder blue with white collar and turnbacks. The front of the coatee and the sleeves were frogged in silver lace. The brass helmet had silver chin scales and a silver helmet plate depicting the Imperial Crown. The brass helmet held a powder blue hair crest on top. The kettle drum banners were of powder blue and embroidered in silver wire with the Eagles and Grenades.

The kettle drummer of the Chasseur à cheval de la Garde in 1806 could be mistaken for that of the Mamelukes, for he was dressed in a surprisingly similar manner. The headdress was a turban with a tall black and white plume, a short blue waistcoat and baggy crimson pantaloons worn with yellow leather boots, around the waist was worn a green and gold sash. The kettle drum banners were of dark green cloth and embroidered in gold with the Imperial coat of arms. The horse harness was covered with gold lace, at the top of the horse's head danced a plume of ostrich feathers in green, silver, white and red.

The Empress's Dragoons of the Imperial Guard in 1810 employed a negro kettle drummer. He wore a light blue uniform and pantaloons tastefully laced in gold with crimson leather boots. His turban was white and surmounted by a plume of red, white and blue ostrich feathers. The

PIPE BAND BASS DRUMS WERE NARROWER THAN THOSE FOR BRASS BANDS.

kettle drums were covered by banners of light blue depicting the Imperial arms. The harness was also covered in gold lace.

The elite Gendarmerie of the Imperial Guard however were a little more restrained, perhaps because of their roll within the guard. The usual bearskin headdress held a red plume on the left side. The 1806 period cutaway coatee was of scarlet cloth laced in silver with blue turnbacks and slashed cuffs also laced in silver. This was worn with buff breeches and black boots. The kettle drum banners were half blue and red, laced in silver with silver fringes and tassels. A silver garter held a gold eagle surmounted by the Crown, the whole was encircled by a wreath of palms.

The Horse Grenadiers of the Guard in 1806 dressed their kettle drummer as a Hussar. He wore an unusual headdress of a cylindrical shape of scarlet cloth without a peak. It was bound with gold lace and covered in a criss cross pattern of gold lace, and a plume of red out of blue feathers completed this extraordinary headdress. The pelisse was dark blue with a dolman crimson edged with white fur. The breeches were crimson and fitted into yellow leather boots. The kettle drum banners were crimson, laced in gold and embroidered with the Imperial coat of arms. The horse harness was just as elaborate, the black leather edged with crimson cloth and held with gilt brass fittings. Between the ears was fastened a large plume of red, white and sky blue ostrich feathers.

With the end of the Napoleonic era the kettle drummers relaxed a little in their dress and appointments. In 1852 the French 8th Hussars had a kettle drummer wearing the uniform of the early part of the Napoleonic era, with a military headdress, pelisse and dolman. The drum banners were white edged in gold. A shield shape badge depicted a stand of red, white and blue colours with a number eight beneath them. Another kettle drummer's uniform of the French Second Empire was most unusual and worn in the 1850's consisted of a chain mail camail and headdress made of gilt chain, a pointed metal helmet also gilt, a surcoat of red cloth. Around the waist was worn a sash of red with gold stripes. The kettle drum banners were dark green with gold lace and fringe. The badge depicted the eagle within a wreath, the saddle cloth was of red cloth, edged in gold lace. This uniform was for the guides of the Imperial Guard and little is known about it or if it was worn as a regular uniform or for a special occasion only.

In Russia and Prussia the kettle drum banners began to form a pattern that was to remain the same as long as horsed units existed. Imperial Germany and the Third Reich also followed the same pattern. The banners were made in three or four sections in an escalloped pattern, each section edged in lace and embroidered with the regimental crest or the royal cypher. Those of the Russian Chevalier Guard in the 1830's were of scarlet cloth edged in silver lace and fringe. The Star of the Order of St. George alternated with the cypher and crown of the Emperor.

Narrow Bass Drum   Rifle Brigade   c.1935
These bass drums were six inches deep and made of brass or aluminium with ash hoops painted in the regimental colours. This particular drum is of the 2nd Battalion the Rifle Brigade (Prince Consort's Own). The background paint would be rifle green.

These banners were not much altered in the following years. By the end of the nineteenth century they were a little longer but of the same pattern. Those of the Empress of Russia's Cuirassiers were of sky blue cloth edged in gold lace and fringe, again the Star Order alternated with the cypher of the Empress in gold embroidery. Before the First World War a French colonial unit, the Senegalese Spahis, employed a kettle drummer whose drums were encased in a red cloth the shape of the drums, these banners were embroidered in yellow silk with a star and crescent. This was quite an unusual style. It was the custom to have draped drum banners or to leave the banners off completely especially if the drums were of silver. There were occasions when silver drums and banners are used such as the British Life Guards and Royal Horse Guards. In Pakistan this practice is followed by the 13th Duke of Connaught's Own Lancers who had silver drums with banners.

DRUM BANNERS 1903

Drum banners are emblazoned with the crest of the regiment and with battle honours. Because lancer and hussar regiments do not have regimental colours, this is the only place they can display the achievements of the regiments. Consequently the drum banners hold an important place as insignia of the band and the regiment.

The other types of cavalry do carry a regimental colour which is called, in the Life Guards and Royal Horse Guards, a 'standard' and a 'guidon' in the Dragoon Guards and Dragoons.

The drum banners are made of cloth edged with gold fringe. The two banners are duplicates of each other, the exception being those of the 21st Empress of India's Lancers, where the off-side banner differs from the nearside. The 3rd King's Own Hussars do not use drum banners at all; their kettle drums are made of silver and inscribed with the regimental crest and battle honours.

Cavalry regiments also had a set of marching-out banners. These were not so elaborate, but they did contain the royal monogram or the regimental badge and were used for parades and for manoeuvres, and when moving from one barracks to another before the days of troop trains.

The kettle drummer would not wear the full dress, but the blue patrol uniform with which was worn the headdress without a plume. Sometimes the pillbox cap would be worn.

Set of Drums
Complete set of drums consisting of eight side drums, two tenor drums and a bass. These were made for an Australian Regiment, 47th Battalion Wide Bay Regiment. These drums are all hand painted with the Australian Coat of Arms with the Regimental Badge below and the Battle Honours each side.

The banners were usually paid for privately and presented, unlike infantry colours. New drum banners were acquired when new honours had been granted or the banners needed replacing.

Drum banners have been illustrated in a colour sheet issued by Messrs Gale and Polden after the First World War and in the Boys' Own Paper in 1903. There have also been three issues of cards by John Player Ltd, all before the First World War; these are very scarce collectors' items. Messrs Raphael Tuck and Sons issued coloured pictures of drum horses early in the reign of King Edward VII.

DRUM HORSE 9th QUEEN'S ROYAL LANCERS 1894

Raised as Dragoons in the reign of George I, they became Lancers in 1816 and during the Indian Mutiny received the nickname 'The Delhi Spearmen'.

The cream coloured filly was presented by Queen Victoria. The forage for this horse and one shilling a week for a man employed to look after it was paid for out of band funds. The horse was named 'Queen Adelaide'. This photograph was taken outside the Riding School at Aldershot.

DRUM HORSE LIFE GUARDS

The Life Guards are the senior regiment of the Household Cavalry. The drum horses are usually skewbald or piebald.

It requires great skill to control this horse, not the least reason being because of the need to control the horse by means of leg reins attached to the stirrup irons, these stirrups are made with a 'D' ring fitting on the outside for the rein to be fastened to. The bit or curb rein is taken over the neck of the horse to within the reach of the drummer, or for use as a bearing rein. The snaffle rein is left loose over the neck of the horse.

The drum horse is taught to stand still for long periods of time and adopts that posture shown in the illustration, with the hind legs stretched out, well back to support the weight of the drums and the kettle drummer.

The silver drums were presented to the Regiment by King William IV at Windsor Great Park in 1831. The drum banners are of figured silk, edged in heavy gold fringe and embroidered in gold and silver wire with the royal coat of arms complete with supporters. At each side is the sovereign's monogram inscribed and reversed with a crown above. The edges of the drum banners are ornamentally embroidered in gold wire, the corners decorated with the rose, shamrock, thistle and leeks in gold wire embroidery.

The shabraque is of scarlet cloth, edged in gold lace and piped each side in scarlet. It is heavily embroidered in gold and silver wire with the Order of the Garter surrounded by an ornamentation of gold and silver wire. There is also a throat plume of black over red. In State dress the kettle drummers of both the Life Guards and the Royal Horse Guards are the same, because they are acting in a State capacity. For other duties they wear their regimentals and are easily distinguishable from one another.

KETTLE DRUM CARRIAGE 1748

This interesting and historic piece of equipment was used in 1772 at the funeral of the first Duke of Marlborough, John Churchill. It was in permanent use by the Royal Artillery until 1756 when it was stored in the Tower of London until it was unfortunately destroyed by fire in the mid-nineteenth century.

The uniforms worn by the driver and the leader and also by the kettle drummer and trumpeters was court livery and not the uniform of the Royal Artillery. The drum major and state trumpeters of the Household Brigade wore a uniform almost identical to that worn to this day by virtue of the fact that they were members of the Royal Household.

The idea and use of the kettle drums mounted on a carriage originated on the continent. It is known that the Prussian army used them around 1690.

That used by the Royal Artillery was pulled by six greys. The wheels of the carriage were painted red and blue, the back panel of wood was covered and gilded, depicting the full royal coat of arms with supporters. The kettle drums themselves were covered by crimson genoa damask drum banners, heavily fringed and tasselled. They were embroidered on the face with the royal coat of arms in gold and silver wire. These imposing items were used during campaigns and were equipped with oil-skin covers for inclement weather. The original drum banners are at the Royal Artillery Headquarters at Woolwich.

A painting depicting these kettle drums in the Low Countries, dated 1748 by David Marier (1705–70), a Swiss artist born in Berne, is in the possession of Her Majesty the Queen. Of great size, it measures 136 cm by 171 cm, and is the largest known painting by this artist. Another feature of this carriage was the fact that the ordnance flag was carried attached to the fore part of the piece. The full size replica was constructed at the Royal Arsenal, Woolwich in 1925 for the Royal Artillery pageant of that year, but the drum banners were not used at this time.

The State dress used by the drummer, leader and driver was of scarlet cloth decorated with broad gold lace and buttons covered over with gold lace. The lace had a blue light between. These are the royal colours and are still in use today, only with slight modifications. The driver wore a tricorn hat of black felt ornamented with gold lace. The leader wore a blue velvet peaked cap. The harness of black leather was ornamented with gilt fittings.

KETTLE DRUMMER ROYAL SCOTS GREYS 1894

The drum horse was named Plum Duff and was purchased in Ireland in 1885 as a five year old. He was so named because of his dark coat which was covered with white spots, however by 1894 the coat had gone white with age. He retired in the late 1890's.

The drum banners were scarlet and embroidered in gold wire with gold lace and fringes. The throat plume was also scarlet as was the bearskin plume of the kettle drummer.

The kettle drummer, A. E. Booth, had joined the regiment in 1876. His father had been band sergeant and an uncle a kettle drummer, both in the Greys.

Kettledrummer   Royal Scots Greys   1894

SINCE THE EARLY 1900'S
BUT TRADITIONALLY, THE DRUM HORSE OF
THE GREYS WAS <u>BLACK</u>

IN THE EARLY 30'S THERE WAS "LAIRDSBURN" FOLLOWED BY "REX" WHO
LEFT ON MECHANISATION 1941

IN 1971 THE QUEEN PRESENTED "A BLACK'UN" (EX. THE H.C.R.) TO
THE ROYAL SCOTS DRAGOON GUARDS (CARABINIERS & GREYS)

FRENCH DRUM 2nd EMPIRE *(Left)*

A French side drum with a brass shell, this had on the side an applied French eagle standing on a bolt of lightning. The eagle was not crowned and may date from the time when Louis Napoleon was President of the French Republic in 1851.

Shako plates of the period clearly show where a crown has been soldered on after the creation of the Second Empire. This apparently was not the case with this particular drum.

At each quarter of the eagle were applied four brass grenades. The hoops were in the national colours, red, white and blue, the cords white with leather fittings.

SCOTS GUARD SIDE DRUM *(Right)*

This drum has a brass shell, painted royal blue, emblazoned on the side is the complete royal coat of arms with supporters. Below is the star of the Order of the Thistle, which James II founded in 1687. Also included is the sphinx resting on a tablet inscribed 'Egypt', this was awarded after the Egyptian campaign of 1801.

Above the coat of arms is a scroll bearing the regimental title. Each side of the coat of arms are listed the many battle honours of the regiment, from Namur in 1695, when it was under the command of King William III. It was also commanded by King George II at Dettingen, the last ~~English~~ King to lead his troops personally in the field.

BRITISH

They fought in the Peninsular campaign and at Waterloo. They suffered the personal hardships of the Crimea.

The uniform has no plume in the bearskin cap, the only Guard Regiment without. The buttons are grouped in threes and the collar badges are in the form of the Scottish thistle. The Colonel of the Regiment is His Royal Highness the Duke of Gloucester.

 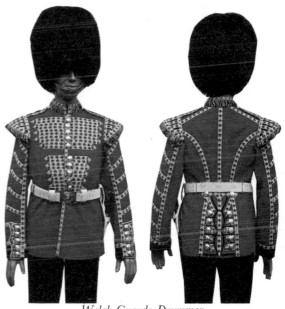

Welsh Guards Drummer

COLDSTREAM GUARDS SIDE DRUM *(Left)*

This shows the Coldstream Guards side drum of the pattern used today, it is hand-painted. The shell is painted royal blue and in the centre is the royal coat of arms complete with supports, above is a scroll bearing the regimental title, below a garter star, the badge of the regiment, flanked by red roses. Below the star is the sphinx and tablet 'Egypt'. On each side of the coat of arms are listed the battle honours of the regiment. To this regiment falls the distinction of having the longest service on the English establishment. It was formed in 1650 under Colonel George Monk, when Oliver Cromwell was preparing for his campaign in Scotland.

On the Restoration this regiment, at Tower Hill, 'grounded arms' and picked them up as 'The Kings Guards'. Colonel Monk was created Duke of Albemarle, for he was largely instrumental in restoring Charles II to the throne. The regimental motto is 'Nulli secundis' meaning 'second to none'. The sphinx was granted for service in Egypt in 1801. They were at

Waterloo where they defended the key position of the Chateau de Hougo-mont. The regiment takes its name from the town of Coldstream on the Scottish side of the river Tweed from which it marched to London in 1660.

WELSH GUARDS DRUMMER *(p.59)*

In 1915 on 25 February, King George V signed the Royal Warrant for the formation of a Regiment of Welsh Guards. Many Welshmen were at this time serving in the Grenadier Guards, but on the signing of the Royal Warrant the colonels of the three other Guard regiments approved the appeal for Welshmen already serving in the Brigade to transfer to the new regiment. On St. Davids Day, 1 March 1915 the Regiment formed the King's Guard at Buckingham Palace for the first time.

Their first battle honour 'Loos', was awarded in that same year. The bearskin of the pattern worn by all the Guards regiments bears a nine inch plume on the left side, made of white feathers with a two inch band of green in the centre. Their buttons are grouped in fives. Although the appeal for Welsh Guardsmen produced 500 men including 40 N.C.O.s, officers were not so plentiful to start with, and a unique record was acquired when on St. David's Day 1915, the first lieutenant-colonel of the Regiment also acted as captain of the King's Guard.

The Corps of Drums are dressed in the same tunic as the other Guards Regiment drummers, except that the buttons are grouped in fives, and the collars are ornamented with the regimental badge, the leek, which also serves as the cap badge.

The tunic for the drummers are laced in the special half inch white drummers lace for Foot Guards, which are woven with a blue fleur-de-lis motif which alluded to the British Sovereign's claim to the kingdom of France, which was finally relinquished by King George III.

3rd KING'S OWN HUSSARS 1895

The kettle drummer is wearing the silver collar presented by Lady South-ampton in 1772 when her husband, Charles Fitzroy, Lord Southampton, was appointed Colonel of the Regiment. It is engraved with military devices and is three and a half inches high.

The drums are of solid silver weighing 1,000 ounces and are supported by three lions paws. Ten lions' heads decorate the drums to hold the skins. The drums date from 1856, the previous set having unfortunately been destroyed by fire.

The shabraque is of the officers' pattern with a leopard skin over the saddle edged in scarlet cloth.

3rd King's Own Hussars 1895

DRUM HORSE 8th KING'S ROYAL IRISH HUSSARS c. 1896

When the 8th King's Royal Irish Hussars returned from India in 1889 new drum banners were obtained to accommodate the battle honours received since 1853. Made of scarlet cloth and bound all round in gold lace, the banners displayed the regimental crest and motto in the centre. The honours, Leswaree, Hindoostan and Alma were of the left, in the centre below the badges, Central India and Afghanistan 1879–80. On the right side were the honours Balaklava, Inkerman and Sebastopol.

The kettle drummer wore the standard hussar uniform, the same as the rest of the Regiment. In 1904 collar badges were worn for the first time. Also in 1904, the saddle acquired a leopard skin cover with a scarlet escalloped edge. The shabraque was of blue cloth with pointed ends, laced all round in gold and bearing on the hindquarters the Irish harp with Queen Victoria's monogram above with the royal crown below. The whole was surrounded by a wreath of laurel and shamrocks. Below the wreath was the number 8 and the letters KRIH. The throat plume was white out of red.

The mounted band took part in the Jubilee Celebrations of Queen Victoria in 1897 and were then stationed in Ireland.

In 1904 a fine skewbald horse called Togo assumed duties as drum horse. In 1909 the regiment sailed for India.

An interesting feature of the colour picture is that the horse is not controlled by the usual reins fitted to the stirrups.

MOUNTED KETTLE DRUMMER 1896
ROYAL ARTILLERY BAND

In 1886, because of the large number of Royal Artillery personnel stationed at Aldershot, the commander-in-chief decided that the Royal Artillery mounted band at Woolwich, the regimental headquarters, was to send twenty-five bandsmen to Aldershot to form a mounted band. The following year the mounted band was complete at Aldershot. The band consisted of a kettle drummer, two trombones, eight cornets, three tenor horns, two euphoniums, two baritones and two E flat bombardons.

The uniform consisted of the black sable busby with a scarlet bag on the right and on the left a brass grenade from which issued a scarlet cut-feather plume. The busby was held to the head by a chin chain of brass. The tunic was the undress patrol jacket of the Royal Artillery. This was of dark blue cloth with a scarlet collar edged in gold lace; at each side on the front were gilt grenade badges. The front of the jacket was piped with gold russia braid and fastened by hooks and eyes. The shoulder straps were gold cords held by a gilt button at the collar. The cuffs were plain dark blue with an austrian knot in gold cord. The pouch belt worn over the left shoulder was white leather with a large black patent leather pouch, which

had the regimental cannon badge in the centre of the flap. The pouch
held the music cards. The waistbelt was of white leather with a brass
snake-hook clasp. No sword was worn in the band, the sword slings being
linked together. White leather gloves were worn for parades.

The riding breeches were dark blue with a broad red stripe down the
outer seam. The riding boots were of black leather. In undress a blue
forage cap with gold lace band was worn.

The silver-plated kettle drums were without drum banners, these being
the prerogative of the Aldershot band, and there was no shabraque. The
harness was of brown leather with a brass-studded bridle and breast plate
of brass depicting the grenade badge. The third or foot rein fastened on to
the stirrups, and with this rein the kettle drummer guided his horse, the
bit and bridle reins resting in the neck. The saddle was the usual army
pattern.

The mounted portion of the Royal Artillery band was abolished in 1897.

ROYAL ARTILLERY DRUM HORSE 1903 *(p.63)*

The Royal Horse Artillery had a mounted band in the early nineteenth
century. In 1877 it was amalgamated with the Royal Artillery to form the
Royal Artillery Mounted Band. In 1886 it was divided into two sections,
one at Woolwich and one at Aldershot. The section at Aldershot carried
drum banners. The drum horse at Woolwich is illustrated elsewhere. The
drum banners of both sections were the same, of dark blue cloth, edged
with a wide gold lace. The fronts were embroidered with the complete
royal coat of arms with supporters, in gold and silver wire. Beneath the
royal arms was a scroll bearing the battle honour 'UBIQUE' (everywhere).
This was because the Royal Artillery had been in practically every action
and certainly every war that the British army had fought. Below this was
the cannon badge and another scroll in three sections with: 'QUO FAS
ET GLORIA DUCUNT'. The busby replaced the helmet in 1895 and the
plume was scarlet goat hair. The grenade of gilt brass which held the plume
was placed at the front instead of the left side. The busby bag was scarlet.

The tunic was of blue cloth, single-breasted with a standing collar,
faced all round in half-inch gold lace. The pointed cuffs were blue and
ornamented with gold lace and russia braid, with a scarlet inset between
the gold lace ornamentations. The tunic was edged in gold cord. The skirts
were rounded at the front with a figured decoration in gold cord. The back
skirts were laced in gold, with russia braid as well.

The pantaloons were of the Royal Horse Artillery pattern with broad
red stripes, and fitted into black leather riding boots. A white leather

pouch belt was worn over the left shoulder, carrying a black leather pouch ornamented with a brass cannon bugle.

In 1904 a girdle was introduced, three inches wide and divided equally into red, blue and red. The N.C.O.'s chevrons were of gold lace on scarlet cloth with a gold embroidered cannon above them, also on scarlet cloth. The saddle cloth was black lambskin with a red scalloped edge. The shabraque was of blue cloth with rounded ends, edged in gold lace with a red piping each side of the lace. On the rear corners the shabraque was embroidered with the royal cypher, above it a crown and below it the regimental cannon and ornamental scroll.

Scots Guards Bass Drum
Made of ash, aluminium or oak for the shell, it is hand painted with the royal arms, the regimental badge, which is the order of the thistle, and the battle honours. The hoops are of ash with Italian hemp rope, weight 17 lb. Henry Potter Ltd. listed these drums at sixteen gns in 1935.

Silver Bass Drum
A silver bass drum of the 8th Gurkha Regiment presented in memory of those that died in the First World War, it was quite a weight for a Gurkha to carry. In solid silver these were priced at over £100 each before the Second World War.

*Royal Horse Guards   Side Drum   c. 1937
Made with a brass shell, fully emblazoned
with the royal arms, regimental title and
battle honours, this drum weighs 8½ lb.
and then cost 8 gns.*

Grenadier Guards Bass Drum

BASS DRUM GRENADIER GUARD 1911

This drum was larger in size than the present pattern used. The shell was made of wood. The hoops were also of wood and painted in a waved red, blue, white stripe. In the centre was painted the royal coat of arms with supporters on a royal blue background, above a scroll was inscribed First Battalion Grenadier Guards. Below was the regimental badge, a grenade. Onto the grenade was painted the royal cypher and crown, in this case, that of George V.

This regiment has belonged to the Royal Household since it was raised, a connection which is denoted by its badge with the royal cypher, a wreath of roses, thistles and shamrocks surround the grenade.

Below are inscribed on scrolls the battle honours of the Grenadier Guards. The earliest honour was Tangier 1680. The regiment had fought at all the famous battles of British history, Blenheim, Dettingen and all the other Marlborough battles, the Peninsular campaign, and Waterloo, the various Egyptian campaigns of the eighties and in South Africa.

The bearskin cap carried a white hair plume on the left side and the buttons were spaced singly.

17th DUKE OF CAMBRIDGE'S OWN LANCERS 1896
This drum horse was reputed to be twenty years old at this date and was taken over from the 11th Prince Albert's Own Hussars when the 11th returned from India in 1890.

The kettle drum banners were blue cloth embroidered in gold wire. The centre badge was a skull and bones in silver metal, a design also carried stirrup irons and breast harness badge.

IN THE REGIMENT, IX ON THE 17"/21" LANCERS THIS IS NOT DESCRIBED ITS A BADGE BUT AS A 'MOTTO'(FROM THE WORDS "DEATH OR GLORY")

3rd PRINCE OF WALES'S DRAGOON GUARDS 1896
The drum horse was a distinctive piebald that had been obtained from the
20th Hussars when the 3rd Dragoon Guards returned to Aldershot from
South Africa. The drums are without banners, these having been stolen
whilst serving in India, previous to their service in South Africa. Drum
banners were obtained in 1897 for Queen Victoria's Diamond Jubilee.

Trumpeter 3rd Field Battery Canadian Artillery 1898

Trumpeter Bishop was instrumental in saving the lives of six men who had been capsized in the St Lawrence river. He was awarded the Royal Canadian Humane Society's medal for "coolness, promptitude and conspicuous bravery". This medal can be seen on his right breast, military medals only were worn on the left breast. On his right hip he carries a bugle, and on his back, partially hidden he carries a trumpet.

TRUMPETERS
AND BUGLERS

Since medieval times it has been the practice to gather together trumpeters to sound fanfares on occasions of pomp. Eventually these were combined with the kettle drums to form the basis of a regimental band. The task of the trumpets and bugles was to pass on the words of command by a call. This, before the Napoleonic Wars, differed from regiment to regiment, creating great difficulties.

German trumpeters, well known for their skill, were employed by other countries. Napoleon retained the services of David Buhl to organise and standardise the French cavalry signals.

TRUMPETS AND BUGLES
Buhl was well known to Napoleon and had played the trumpet since he was ten years old. He had dedicated 28 trumpet calls to the Emperor, some of which are used by the French army to this day. In 1811 Buhl established a school for trumpeters and buglers under the patronage

IN THE BRITISH CAVALRY ALL FIELD CALLS WERE MADE ON THE (RAUCOUS) BUGLE. CALLS IN CAMP, BARRACKS AND MOUNTED CEREMONIAL ON THE TRUMPET.

E.G. ON THE MARCH, THE CHARGE ETC. P.T.O.

EXCEPT WHEN USE THE TRUMPET HAS CARRIED SLUNG ACROSS THE TRUMPETER'S
BACK AND THE BUGLE CARRIED ON THE RIGHT HAND. SEE PAGES 69, 70 & 131

of Napoleon so that the calls could be standardised and these included
the Drummers as well. Twenty-four students from each regiment of
Grenadiers, Chasseurs and Fusiliers and 48 students from each regiment of
Tiralleurs and Voltigeurs were enrolled to the new school.

The bugle or bugle horn, as it was called, was an innovation introduced
to the army for signalling purposes, but its tone attracted it to the military
bands where it appeared towards the end of the eighteenth century.

The light infantry had bugles from their formation, the rifle regiments

TRUMPETERS
~~Buglers~~ *in Ceylon 1901*
*The Englishman on the right belongs to the Ceylon Volunteer Artillery and is wearing
the lightweight khaki uniform with the 1877 pattern helmet. Metal grenades on the collar
denote artillery.*
                                        TRUMPETER
*On the left a native of Ceylon who is a ~~bugler~~ in the regular Ceylon Native Artillery is
wearing the same uniform with the exception of the headdress.*

Bugler Mounted Infantry 1905
A mounted bugler of the Grenadier Guards Mounted Infantry section is seen here wearing the ill-famed Broderick cap, introduced in 1905 and named after the Minister for War. He is wearing the scarlet drummer's jacket, corduroy breeches, puttees and boots. Over the left shoulder can be seen an ammunition bandolier.

had a complete band of these instruments which were in B flat and gave eight notes and were used throughout armies for the use of giving commands. The calls are the same on both trumpet and bugle, except that those on the trumpet are lower.

Buglers and trumpeters have always been serving members of their regiments, and not counted as being in the band, but soldiers whose station was beside their colonel, so that they could pass on his commands by a call on the trumpet or bugle.

Many are the heroes amongst these men and boys, such as Bugler Dunne of the Royal Dublin Fusiliers who, although wounded, stayed on with his regiment throughout the fearful battle of Colenso. He was only fifteen years old and was, of course, made a great hero. When he landed in England, Queen Victoria sent for him, and the only favour he asked was to be sent back to the front. The Queen presented him with a silver bugle to replace the one that was lost at Colenso in 1899.

The Cavalry Trumpeters were the idol of the mounted bands, where they played in times of peace, but of course their place was by the side of the Colonel during battle to enable him to pass on his orders. The dress of trumpeters became almost theatrical in the use of the most brilliant coloured clothes. The facing was often of several woven colours or used as gold face similar to the officers. During the Napoleonic Wars these uniforms perhaps reached the zenith in the French Cavalry. Some of the uniforms appeared garish, others assumed a quiet elegance such as the

The Victorian Permanent Artillery   Australia   1899
This was a volunteer artillery unit raised in the State of Victoria, Australia. The band at this time was thirty men strong, and was modelled on those in England. The drum major is seen wearing review order. The white helmet is ornamented with a grenade badge. The tunic is adorned with bars of lace. The mace is decorated with a grenade, popular with artillery and engineer regiments.
The boys are wearing the 'Pillbox' caps in place of the white helmets. The bandsman on the right carries both a trumpet and a bugle.
It is interesting to note that the drum major is wearing high heels and placed on a step to increase his height for this photograph.

French Bugler

Empress's Dragoons dressed in white, faced sky blue with gold lace; their plumes were also sky blue and also the saddle cloths.

It was the custom to reverse the colours of the regimental uniform for trumpeters and the band, thus a regiment dressed in blue with green collar and cuffs would dress the musicians in green uniforms with blue collars and cuffs. The headdress and plumes would also be embellished. The French Mounted Grenadiers wore a bearskin headdress. In the band a white bearskin headdress was assumed. This type of dress for trumpeters

Bugler   Sierra Leone Frontier Police   1901
The police in this part of Africa acted as a
military force in a very difficult climate and
terrain, tribal wars and cattle stealing made
worse by crocodile-infested rivers and dark,
sweltering jungles. The medal the bugler is
wearing is for active service in this area.

and the band could be seen all over Europe. A well dressed band was good publicity and helped with recruiting by its dashing uniform. In the United States of America the bands and trumpeters followed the European fashion. The Militia Units were especially colourful, not only in the dress of the soldiers but those of the band. In Russia, where the bands were considered the best in Europe at the beginning of the nineteenth century, the cavalry trumpeters were finely dressed. The trumpeters of the Chevalier Guards after the Napoleonic Wars were dressed in helmets with a red crest, white coatees, heavily frogged with gold lace. These Russian trumpets were without banners and were decorated with silver cords and tassels. The steel breastplate or cuirass was not worn by trumpeters because of the restriction to the chest. This was a common custom throughout Europe and can be seen in practice even today when one watches the Band of the British Life and Horse Guards. Although on state occasions the trumpeters wear state dress and are part of the Royal Household and not part of the regiment.

The bugle was used in the Jäger or Rifle Regiments to pass on the words of command, also by a whistle carried on the officers' pouch belts. These originated in Austria, drawn from the forestry employees, because of the marksmanship. The hunting horn is the badge of these regiments and were quickly adopted by the European powers. Because of their role as light troops and camouflaged in green uniform the bands composed mainly of buglers, had little scope for the exotic uniforms of their compatriots in the other branches of the services.

In modern times, with the disappearance of full dress uniforms except for Guard Units, the bands are the only link with the past glories of the regimental dress, for these are fitted out with full dress of the period before the Second World War. The Italian Bersaglieri were formed in 1836 and is a rifle regiment, like its British counterparts marches at a very fast rate to the accompaniment of bugles. The Italians move at a trot whereas the British march at 140 paces to the minute.

A crack unit of Austrian Jägers was the 26th Battalion. The buglers

Colonel and Bugler 12th Spanish Infantry 1898
The Infantry of the Line consisted of seventy-four regiments, each of two battalions.
This photograph shows the colonel and the bugler. Every Spaniard was at this time obliged to serve three years in the service. Note the oilskin covers to the shakos and the elaborate Austrian knot on the sleeve of the bugler who is wearing the typical Spanish footwear.

were dressed in light blue grey tunics with grass green collar, cuffs and shoulder straps, a black felt hat with a wide brim curving up at the sides, a green cord around the base of the hat with small tassels. The plume was green cock feathers. The bugles were of brass and festooned with green cords and tassels. The badge was a hunting horn which is an allusion to Jäger which means 'hunter', hence the hunting horn.

The sounding of retreat on bugles every evening has its origin as far back as the sixteenth century. A seventeenth century reference to the call is to be found in a British Army Order dated 18th June 1690 in a book of an officer in the Army of James II which states, 'The General to beate att 3 clock in ye morning, ye retreat to beate att 9 att night and take it from ye gards'.

At the sounding of the Last Post by the trumpeters of the 10th Prince of Wales' Own Hussars it is the custom to follow with the regimental march 'God Bless the Prince of Wales' and 'God Save the Queen'. Before the Second World War this was played every night wherever the regiment was stationed, but now they are played on Sunday nights and on special days only. In the 12th Lancers after the bugles have sounded the 'Last Post', the band plays 'The Sicilian Vespers', 'The Former Russian Imperial National Anthem', 'God Bless the Prince of Wales' and 'God Save the Queen'. The custom of playing the first hymn dates from when a party of officers visited the Pope in 1794 and His Holiness presented the hymn.

The Lancashire Fusiliers landed at Gallipoli from H.M.S. Euryalus under a withering fire, six Victoria Crosses were won in this action and later the ship's bell was presented to the regiment in 1934 by the Lords Commissioners of the Admiralty and since then has been used to sound ship's time daily at the barracks. During the Second World War, H.M.S. Euryalus and the 11th Battalion the Lancashire Fusiliers served together in Malta. To commemorate this period the regiment was presented with a silver bugle with royal navy blue dress cords and tassels.

The soldiers' awakening is the reveille, sounded by the Buglers. This is of course the least pleasant call to the soldier and some Commanding Officers of British Regiments decided to substitute something a little brighter. The 6th Carabiniers play a Viennese folk song 'Ach du Lieber Augustin' which is played on six B Flat cornets in three part harmony, two cornets to each part. This was adopted in 1895. The 12th Royal Lancers have since 1898, when stationed near the Carabiniers and hearing the cheerful tune, played their own version, composed by their bandmaster at that time – Mr. Gruare. This has been played ever since.

FRENCH INFANTRY OF THE LINE   TRUMPETER OF THE VOLTIGEURS 1830

The French infantry was much increased under King Louis Phillipe. The uniforms took on a more comfortable aspect, at least with those previously worn.

The trumpeter's shako was of black felt bound at the top with red lace and at the bottom with black leather. The peak was a more square shape than previously. The chin scales of brass were stamped out in one piece and mounted on leather, not individual brass scales as before. The double pompom was of yellow wool. The rosette was in the new national colours of red, white and blue. Beneath this was a brass cockerel standing on a globe, pierced with the regimental number.

The blue coatee had been introduced in 1820, and was single-breasted, fastened by a row of brass buttons. The open collar was red with an edging of bound lace of mixed red, white and blue. The epaulettes were made of yellow cloth with yellow woollen fringes; they were fastened to the shoulder by a brass button. The red cuffs had an edging of the red, white and blue bound lace, the slashes were blue piped red and fastened by three brass buttons, and the coatee turnbacks were red.

The red trousers that were to be a distinctive feature of the French army for the next ninety years were introduced in 1829

French Infantry Trumpeter 1830

The overcoat was grey, carried rolled in a white and grey striped cover on the top of the pack. This equipment was fitted to the soldier by white leather straps. The left shoulder strap supported the bayonet and the right, the black leather ammunition pouch and short sword; this was in the Roman pattern and had an all-brass hilt. It was carried in a black leather scabbard with brass mounts.

The trumpeter carried his musket on the right arm, barrel to the front. The trumpet was decorated with red, white and blue cords with red tassels. This instrument was used not so much as part of the band, but to give signals to the regiment from the commanding officer.

It was during this period that the conquest of North Africa began. The French army was increased in size and began also to create an image of quality, not lost until the Franco-Prussian War, forty years on.

Holstein Artillery Trumpeter 1835

HOLSTEIN ARTILLERY TRUMPETER 1835
The trumpeters' shako was of black felt, bound at the top and bottom with black leather, the peak being bound with brass. The chin scale bosses were in the form of brass lion heads and the chin scales themselves were made of brass. The pom-pom at the top of the shako was of blue worsted wool. The

brass plate at the front was further ornamented by a loop of gold lace that terminated at the pom-pom.

The coatee was of scarlet cloth with a plain blue standing collar. The plastron front was fastened with seven brass buttons on each side, but the coatee was fastened up the centre by means of hooks and eyes. The epaulettes were of blue cloth edged with gold lace, the crescents brass. The band wings worn underneath the epaulettes were blue edged in gold lace and decorated with vertical stripes of gold lace. The cuffs were blue with pointed gold lace edges.

The pouch belt was carried over the left shoulder and was of white leather. The sword belt worn around the waist was also of white leather with a brass snake hook fastening. The sword hung from the left side, suspended by white leather straps. The sword had a brass three-barred half-basket hilt. The scabbard was steel and the sword knot black leather. The overalls were of blue cloth.

The cavalry trumpet was of brass and carried by means of yellow and red twisted cords. The body of the bugle was bound in this cord and ornamented with two tassels in the same materials. The trumpet is the 'natural' pattern, having no mechanical devices or valves, and is coiled to make it easier to manage on horseback. Illustrations of this type of cavalry trumpet appear elsewhere in this book *(p.20)*.

12th Soudanese Regiment 1898
These three buglers and a drummer belong to the Egyptian army. The field officers were British and the Company officers were native Soudanese, on the style of the British Indian Army.
This battalion was at this time commanded by Major Townsend, and fought throughout the Soudan Campaign of 1898

The trumpeters' mounts were white, the harness of black leather with white metal fittings. The shabraque was of blue cloth with pointed ends. It was bound with yellow lace and bore the grenade badge of the artillery and the monogram and crown of the King of Denmark.

TRUMPETER, 13th HUSSARS 1902

Trumpeters of the British cavalry regiments at this time wore virtually the same uniform as the troopers.

The busby had a white bag ornamented with yellow cord on the right hand side. The plume was white horse hair, in a brass plume holder. Yellow cap lines encircled the busby and hung down from under the bag, passing under the left arm up to the right breast, where they were fastened. The dark blue tunic had a white collar, an unusual feature of this regiment, with five rows of yellow cord frogging. The fasteners were brass ball buttons and not olivets as on the officer's tunic. The trumpeter's rank badge on the right upper arm was of white cloth and showed crossed trumpets. The cuffs were plain blue, ornamented with yellow cord austrian knots. The riding breeches were dark blue with double white stripes down the outer seam. The trumpet was always carried in the right hand, the reins in the left.

13th Hussars

TRUMPET MAJOR

The cavalry regiments had one sergeant trumpeter and eight trumpeters, one for each troop. The commanding officer's trumpeter rode at his side *ON THE BUGLE* and was used to sound orders to the regiment in times of emergency. In and around the camp the trumpeters called out the day-to-day duties of the regiment. *TRUMPETS*

THE VETERAN 1894

The bugler in the centre belongs to the Coldstream Guards and is wearing the white drill jacket, his white leather belt supports the band sword seen on his left hip. The drummer boy on the right is from the Grenadier Guards and is wearing the scarlet tunic with white lacing. The band sword can be clearly seen. The Chelsea Pensioner's uniform has not altered from that date. The medal they are admiring is for service in the Crimea War of 1855.

Royal Artillery Band 1847

THE BAND
AND
THE BANDMASTER

The first military bands were raised in Germany and were paid for by the officers of the regiment or by the individual State.

In England the first regimental band was that of the Royal Artillery in 1762. Before this period bands were only raised for a special purpose or occasion, and then disbanded. The bands gradually spread throughout the armies, and were at first paid for by the officers, and eventually by the State.

The use of the band was to add pomp and military bearing to a regiment on the march, and also keep these men in step. Much money was expended on the bands, and the uniforms often had no resemblance to those of the regiment it was leading. One American regiment in the early part of the nineteenth century were led by a band dressed as lancers.

The bandmaster, who was at first a civilian, was paid by the officers, and the wealthier the officers, the better was the band. Later, in the nineteenth century these bandmasters were serving members of the regiment and held a commissioned rank. Many became famous as writers of marches, some, such as Sousa, became world famous, and, as the taste for military music spread, performed concerts for the general public. Sunday concerts became a fashionable meeting place for officers and their friends. These were held in parks, which made an ideal setting in the days before the First World War. Later, this more leisurely life was swept away.

ROYAL ARTILLERY BAND 1847

In 1844 a new headdress was adopted by the Royal Artillery in place of the bell-topped shako. This was the sealskin cap with a scarlet plume of hair on the left hand side and held by a patent leather chin-strap.

The coatee was introduced in 1839, similar to that worn by the troops except the lacing was gold and not yellow worsted. The collar was scarlet, laced all round in gold, the dark blue coatee was double-breasted and fastened by two rows of nine buttons in each row. The rounded cuffs were scarlet and had dark blue slashes piped in gold and fastened by three brass buttons. The leading edge of the coatee was piped scarlet and the turn-backs and tails were of the same colour. The coat tails were laced in gold all round to the waist. At the waist was carried a band sword. This had an all brass hilt and a black leather scabbard with brass mountings. These had been presented by the Duke of Kent, father of Queen Victoria.

The drummers at this period continued to wear scarlet coatees until 1851 when they were issued with blue.

The overalls were dark blue with a broad scarlet stripe down the outer seam. Light blue trousers were abolished in 1847 and the dark blue adopted also. The drummers were then dressed as the rank and file in practically

Indian Army "*The Drums*"

all features. The Royal Artillery was the last regiment in the army to have the drummers, fifers and trumpeters in the colour of the regimental facings.

The drum major continued to wear the scarlet coatee and the bearskin cap with scarlet plume. His light blue trousers were also substituted by the dark blue pattern in 1847.

The bandsman at the front of the picture is depicted with the ophicleide, an instrument very popular with brass bands and with resonant tone. It was called the chromatic bullock, but remained popular until the end of the nineteenth century. The large keyhole covers were called saucepan lids, amongst other names.

BANDMASTER, BAND CORPORAL AND MUSICIANS 1856
During the Crimean War a Victoria Cross was won by a Royal Artillery bandsman, Andrew Henry, who was the principal keyed bugle player in the band. A flügelhorn player, John McLaren, won the French Military Medal. Andrew Henry was later commissioned and reached the rank of captain in the Coast Artillery Brigade, but John McLaren died later as a result of his privations in the War.

At the end of the Crimean War a black sable busby was adopted by the band; this had a scarlet bag on the right side, and on the left, a gilt brass grenade bearing the regimental crest and a scarlet hackle feather plume which reached to the top of the busby.

The coatee was abolished and a tunic adopted, of dark blue cloth, with scarlet collar with rounded ends, laced all round in gold. The tunic was single-breasted and fastened with hooks and eyes, but the front was decorated with five bars of broad gold lace, three-quarters of an inch wide and edged with a tracery of gold russia braid. The cuffs were dark blue, laced in gold, with a similar tracery of gold russia braid. Along the back seams was piping of gold lace and gold russia braid. The blue shoulder straps were edged in gold and embroidered on the top with a grenade. On each forearm, immediately above the cuff, was worn a gold-embroidered lyre with silver wire strings.

The trousers were of dark blue with broad scarlet stripes down the outer seam. The band sergeant and sergeants wore one-and-three-quarter-inch gold lace stripes on the trousers and three gold lace chevrons on the arm, surmounted by the regimental cannon in gold wire. In 1859 the band sergeant's stripes were increased to four. The bandmaster wore an officer's pouch belt of gold lace on blue morocco leather with an embroidered pouch and an officer's pattern sword in a steel scabbard.

The band continued to wear the side arms that they had worn with the previous uniform. In undress a blue peaked cap was worn with a gold lace band and an embroidered button on the top in gold.

In 1857 the Military School of Music at Kneller Hall was established, supported voluntarily by the regiments, although the Royal Artillery continued to train their own bandsmen, they continued to subscribe generously.

The drum major's staff was the same as that used previously with a gilt head and gilt encircling chains ending in two gold tassels. In 1860 the drum major was further dignified by wearing a sword. James Lowerie retired from his post in 1861, and the position lapsed. Also in 1861 the regimental band's patron, the Duchess of Kent, died. She, it is claimed, wrote the Royal Artillery Slow March for the Regiment.

AUSTRO-HUNGARIAN GERMAN INFANTRY
BANDSMEN 1859

The drum major of the German infantry of the Austro-Hungarian army wore an officer's pattern shako of tapering black felt, bound at the top with two rows of gold lace and at the bottom with black leather. The black leather peak was bound with brass. At the top of the shako a gold cord button bore in the centre, the monogram of the Emperor Franz Joseph. The shako badge was the Austrian eagle made in brass.

Austro-Hungarian

The double-breasted tunic was white, the colour of the Imperial Army for many years. The collar was green, edged at the front and bottom with gold lace. Rank stars decorated the front. The rounded cuffs were green and fastened with two brass buttons at the back. The tunic was fastened by two rows of eight brass buttons. The shoulder straps were yellow, bound in gold lace and had yellow woollen tufted ends. The band wings were made of vertical stripes of gold lace with a black light in between. Yellow and black were the national colours. The trousers were of light blue cloth with a white piping down the outer seams. The drum major's sash worn over the right shoulder was of green cloth and edged in an escalloped edged silver lace. The same lace decorated the centre of the sash. The sash was further embellished by two black ebony drum sticks with gilt mounts fastened to the centre of the sash.

The drummer wore the infantryman's shako of tapering black felt, bound at the top and bottom with black leather, the peak not being bound. The badge at the front was the Austrian eagle in brass. The yellow circular ball at the top of the shako bore the monogram of the Emperor. The white cloth tunic had a standing collar in the regimental facing colour and was edged in white lace at the front and lower edge. The shoulder straps were in the facing colour and edged in white. The wings were also edged in an escalloped edged white lace. The cuffs were fastened with two brass buttons and had an edging of white lace at the top and back edge. The tunic was piped on the leading edge in the facing colour and fastened by two rows of eight brass buttons. The trousers were light blue and had piping of white down the outer seam.

The drum was carried on a white shoulder strap over the right shoulder. The drum was of brass with wooden hoops painted black and yellow, the national colours. From a belt over the same shoulder, the drummer carried the short sword with a stirrup hilt of brass, which was issued to all infantry. It was in a leather and brass scabbard.

Trumpeters were dressed in the same manner with the cords of yellow and black, to carry the trumpet.

BRITISH INFANTRY BAND c. 1896
Regiments on the march were always led by the fifes and drums. It is always easier to march to the band, and to keep in step. When the

regiment was soon to stop for a rest or break, the fifes and drums would strike up 'Polly put the kettle on'.

The bandsman as shown here wore the same equipment as the other soldiers, minus the ammunition pouches on the waistbelts. The bandsman's sword was worn in place of the bayonet.

The fifers wore their bugles at the right hip from green cords slung over the left shoulder. The haversack of white canvass and the water bottle were carried on the left hip by shoulder straps. The valise was worn on the back by 'D' rings on the braces and fastened to double buckles on the front above the belt. The mess tin in an oilskin cover was strapped to the rolled blanket, which was fastened to the waistbelt at the back. The haversack contained emergency rations, and this was carried by all, including the band.

For marching order, the men wore black leather leggings with four eyelets for fastening down the sides.

The two mounted officers shown were the commanding officer and a major.

BAND CORPORAL (CONCERT DRESS) MUSICIAN AND BAND-MASTER 1910 ROYAL ARTILLERY BAND

In 1895 the busby was re-introduced for the band. It was made of black seal skin with a scarlet bag on the right side, practically the same as that worn in the 1850's and 60's. The grenade badge was moved to the front and a scarlet horse-hair plume adopted in place of the plume of feathers previously worn. A gilt chain chin strap was used in place of the patent leather strap.

In 1908 a dark blue forage cap with a peak was issued; this had a scarlet band and welts. The badge at the front was in brass and depicted the regimental crest. This headdress was worn at concerts and other indoor or informal occasions.

The tunic was the same as previously worn, with scarlet collar, gold laced, and five rows of broad gold lace across the chest, edged in a gold russia piping, ending at the skirt with austrian knots. In 1908 the loose trousers were replaced by tight fitting blue overalls with broad scarlet stripes along the outer seam. These overalls buttoned under the shoes. The bandmaster had a black sealskin busby with a scarlet bag on the right side and a gilt grenade badge at the front. His plume was made of scarlet feathers and was of the same size and proportions as that worn by officers of the Royal Horse Artillery. His tunic was of blue cloth with a scarlet collar laced all round with gold. Within the collar was a decoration of twisted gold cord of the pattern on the officer's full-dress tunic.

Bandmaster, Band Corporal and Musician

The tunic was single-breasted and fastened by hooks and eyes. On each side of the opening was broad gold lace, edged with four panels of gold russia braid in a formal austrian knot design. The cuffs were laced in gold of the pattern used for the officer's full-dress uniform. The pouch belt was gold lace on blue morocco leather. The pouch was black patent leather with a gilt brass regimental badge on the flap. The overalls were dark blue with a broad gold stripe down the outer seam. The bandmaster carried a sword of the officer's pattern with gold sword knot.

In undress the bandmaster wore a frock coat of dark blue with five rows of black silk frogging and olivets. The peaked cap was worn in this order of dress. For the bandsmen, for training and practice, a blue serge jacket was introduced with patch pockets and brass buttons. Only the forage cap was worn with this jacket.

The bandsman at the back is playing the saxophone, and the one in the centre of the picture is holding a euphonium.

ROYAL ARTILLERY BAND 1953

After the Second World War, drab khaki was the only garb of the band
until the year 1950 when all blue tunics, trousers and peaked caps appeared, with brass buttons in place of hooks and eyes of the previous
years. By 1951, the band attained a little more colour to the uniform, this
consisted of the blue peaked cap with a red band and red welts, and the
regimental cap badge in brass. The tunic was blue cloth, single-breasted
and fastened by a row of five brass buttons. The standing collar was red
with a narrow lace in gold all round. A grenade was placed each side on
the collar. The shoulder straps were replaced by gold shoulder cords with a
brass button fastening. The scarlet cuffs were pointed, with austrian knots
in gold cord. A gold thread lyre was embroidered on the forearm. The
N.C.O.'s stripes were in gold lace. A girdle round the waist was adopted

in place of the plain blue belt. This was in the regimental colours, red, yellow and blue. The buckle in the front was eventually moved to the side

In 1950 the band sword was also re-instated and worn on the left side from a frog fitting. Later the peaked cap was abolished and the band re-adopted the sealskin busby with a red bag on the right side and the grenade at the front, holding the scarlet plume.

Coldstream Guards 1894
2nd Lieutenant Heathcote-Amory of 1st Battalion Coldstream Guards was the tallest officer at six foot and one and a quarter inches tall. The drummer is John Marshall, an orphan, picked up by the regiment on manoeuvres near Swindon in 1893, whilst following the troops.
The officers of the regiment placed him in the Gordon's Boys School, there he became a cornet player from whence he was received into the 1st Coldstream Guards as a drummer boy.

 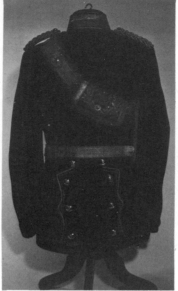 

Bandmasters Tunic 1966 (Front)   Bandmasters Tunic 1966 (Back)   Bandmasters Tunic

BANDMASTER'S TUNIC ROYAL ARTILLERY 1966

The bandmaster's tunic is that accorded to Royal Artillery officers in the 1911 dress regulations. It is of blue cloth with a standing collar of scarlet cloth, square in front, but slightly rounded at the corners and fastened with two hooks and eyes, the collar being edged all round in gold cord with lace one and a sixteenth of an inch wide round the top within the cords. The cuffs are dark blue with austrian knots of gold cord eight and a quarter inches from the bottom of the cuff. The skirt is cut square at the front, open behind with a blue slash on the back of each skirt. The slashes are piped on the edge with gold cord and traced inside with gold russia braid, the skirts being lined with black. Scarlet cloth edging is down the front and at the opening behind. There are nine gilt buttons down the front, two at the waist and three on each slash, plaited gold wire shoulder cords, lined with blue fastened by a small regimental button.

The sword belt is of gold lace one and a half inches wide lined with blue morocco leather and fastened with a gilt snake hook inscribed 'ubique' joining two oval gilt plates, each bearing the royal crest.

The shoulder belt is of gold lace two inches wide, lined with blue morocco leather with an ornamental buckle and slide and a grenade within a wreath at the end. The pouch is of black leather with gilt fitting. The flap is of blue cloth edged with gold lace and in the centre the royal coat of arms with below, the regimental badge. The whole is surrounded by a wreath of laurels.

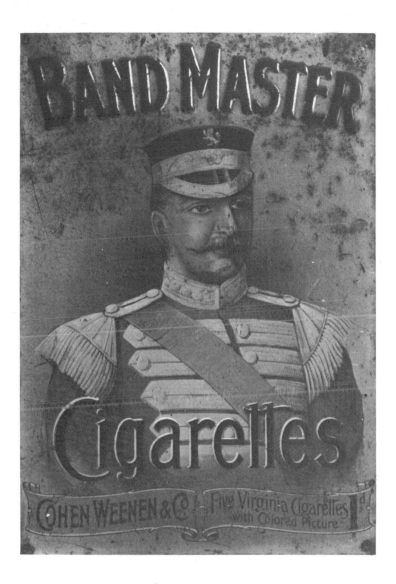

CIGARETTE ADVERTISEMENT c. 1900

This advertisement for Bandmaster cigarettes dates from about the turn of the century. Although the army has always been popular with the advertising media, this is the only one known to be of a bandsman, others being usually of general military interest.

The lion and rose on the Bandmaster's forage cap could refer to the King's Royal Lancaster Regiment. With the royal blue facings this would be correct. The advertisement is in enamelled tin, of the type often used on railway stations.

PRUSSIA HORNIST 3rd RIFLE BATTALION SCHELLENBAUM
BEARER 13th INFANTRY 1835

The Prussians shown are wearing the shako, introduced in 1816, that was
to last until the adoption of the pickelhaube in 1843. This was of black felt
bound in black leather. The chin scales were of brass overlapping plates.
The cockade was in the national colours of Prussia, black and white.
From the centre front of the shako a black rosette with a brass button held
a stripe of yellow lace which went up to the cockade. Across the front of the
shako white twisted cords were held at each side of the top of the shako by
small hooks; from the right side fell white cords with white tassels and
flounders. The French horn player is shown in a similar shako with the
full dress plume of red with a white top.

The coatee of both regiments was of the same cut and pattern, the 13th Infantry having Prussian blue cloth, double breasted and fastened by a row of brass buttons. The facings were red, the standing collar was laced at the front and top edge with a gold lace. The red cuffs had a gold lace edge. The slashes were white with a three button fastening. The shoulder straps were blue and embroidered with the regimental number. The band wings were of red cloth with vertical stripes of gold lace and a red and gold fringe end. The turnbacks of the coatee were red. The trousers were of white linen, worn with white buttoned gaiters and black boots.

Over the right shoulder was worn a white leather belt to support the schellenbaum. This was carried at the head of the band. The staff was of black wood at the head, the black Prussian eagle with a gilt crowned head holding in its beak, by means of a silver chain, a banner embroidered in gold wire with a wreath of laurels and the monogram of King Frederick William. The banner itself was edged in gold fringing. Beneath the eagle was a brass sunburst, and below that a white metal crescent, at each end a brass eagle's head, holding in its beak a horsehair plume, one red and the other white. Beneath the crescent a decoration of oak leaves ended in a large white metal bell heavily chased and engraved with oak leaves. Around the edge of the large bell were hung small bells and stars. The exotic item depicted was in fact purchased by officers of the regiment, or sometimes by the inhabitants of the garrison town. This instrument is still in use today having survived the two World Wars.

THE BORDER REGIMENT c. 1896
The helmet badge was composed of a Maltese Cross, on the four arms were inscribed eleven battle honours. The cross was superimposed on a laurel wreath, in the centre was a circle inscribed 'Arroyo dos Molinos 1811'. In the centre of the circle was a dragon. The lower part of the centre was voided to show a red cloth backing.

The tunics were scarlet with yellow facings. The helmets were the blue cloth pattern introduced in 1878, on the creation of county regiments. In 1881 the regimental badge, described above, replaced the regimental number that was used in the centre of the helmet.

It was at Arroyo dos Molinos that the 34th Foot, later 1st Battalion, the Border regiment captured the French 34th Regiment and they still have in their possession the drum major's staff and drums of that French regiment.

The regimental march of the regiment is 'John Peel', said to have been written by John Woodcock Graves in about 1829 to a folk tune 'Bonnie Annie'. The original John Peel died in 1854, and was a Cumberland

British Drummers
Border Regiment 1896

yeoman who for 55 years maintained a pack of hounds at Caldbeck where he was born and lived all his life.

The drum major's sash was gold laced and bore in the centre the regimental crest. The scrolls depicted the various battle honours.

These items together with the drum major's staff were presented by the officers who often paid for the upkeep of the band.

On occasions the county would present items, a favourite being a set of silver drums. The Border Regiment received white facings in 1881, but later reverted to their original yellow facings.

The regimental colours bear witness to the many campaigns that the battalions have fought, these included Gibraltar, Fontenoy, the North American campaigns, the Peninsular campaigns, the Crimea and Indian Mutiny and South Africa.

PRINCE ALBERT'S SOMERSET LIGHT INFANTRY c. 1896
This regiment was formed in 1685 by Theophilus, 7th Earl of Huntingdon, at the request of King James II. In 1842 it was formed into a Light Infantry Regiment. The next alteration came in 1882 when, because of its conduct in the 1st Afghan War, the Queen was graciously pleased to approve of the regiment assuming the title 'Prince Albert's Regiment of

Prince Albert's Light Infantry 1896

Light Infantry', and the facing colours were changed to royal blue. A mural crown superinscribed 'Jellalabad' was added to the colours, drums and appointments. The regimental march had a tradition that it was composed by Prince Albert himself, but apparently it was the work of a German bandmaster, J. II. Walch, who came from Prince Albert's Principality, Coburg.

The only difference between light infantry and infantry of the line regimental uniforms was the helmet, which was covered in a dark green cloth for light infantry. The helmet plate in brass of an eight pointed star with a crown at the head depicted in the centre a stringed bugle horn surmounted by a mural crown with a scroll above inscribed 'Jellalabad'. The sphinx on a tablet inscribed 'Egypt' lay between the bugle horns. The scarlet tunic had blue facings. The buglers had the addition of wings, with green bugle horns. The belts were of white leather with brass fittings. The trousers were dark blue with red stripes on the outer welts. The regiment fought at Dettingen, and was at Culloden in 1746. During the Napoleonic Wars the regiment was fighting in the West Indies. It served in India for most of the Victorian period. They were also present at the Crimea and the Boer War.

ROYAL MARINE LIGHT INFANTRY c. 1896
It was decided to present a new colour to each of the four Royal Marine divisions in 1827, and King George IV was presented with a list of 106

actions from which to choose those that should be emblazoned on the colours. This, however was an impossible task, so the King directed 'That the globe circled with laurel should be the distinguishing badge as the most appropriate emblem of the corps whose duties carried them to all parts of the globe in every quarter of which they had earned laurels by their valour and good conduct'. The King's cypher was also carried and the motto 'per mare per terram' meaning 'by sea, by land'. The fouled anchor represents the Admiralty and Gibraltar to commemorate the capture and defence of that position. These were the badges used to ornament the helmet plates and the drum major's sashes. They were also displayed on the drums.

The scarlet tunics had slashed cuffs similar to the Brigade of Guards with royal blue facings, and about this period began to wear the white helmet for ceremonial duties, a custom carried on to this day. The regimental march is 'A life on the ocean wave'. The words are from a poem by Epps Sargent, and the march was adopted by the Royal Marines in about 1880. Lord Mountbatten who was appointed Colonel Commandant of the Royal Marines for life in 1965, introduced the Russian march the 'Preobrajensky' as the regimental slow march. His uncle Grand Duke Serge was one of the last colonels of the Russian Preobrajensky Guards, and the music was adopted as the regimental slow march in 1965. The Royal Marine Light Infantry Band, Portsmouth division, had as an additional badge, the white rose of York, to commemorate the band's attendance on His Royal Highness the Duke of York, later George VI, on his voyage to the Colonies in 1901.

Royal Welsh Fusiliers

ROYAL WELSH FUSILIERS c. 1896

The fusilier who supervises the goat on ceremonial occasions is called the Goat Major. The horns of the goat were encased in polished brass, and he wore a silver shield on his forehead, engraved with the name of the sovereign who presented him to the regiment. The mascot goat has been on the strength of the regiment since 1775, when it was recorded that the regimental goat was present at the Battle of Bunker Hill.

At one time a drummer boy rode the goat around the table at the officers mess on St David's Day during the distribution of the leeks. However on one occasion the drummer boy was flung upon the table and killed by the goat, and the practice was discontinued.

The fusilier cap was made of raccoon skin, the badge at the front was a brass grenade, bearing the crest of the Prince of Wales on the ball. The scarlet jacket had royal blue facings, the gold lace used by officers is of the English pattern with a woven rose design. The drummers' red jackets were laced with white drummers lace along the seams. They also had bandsmen's wings with fringed ends. The buttons were brass bearing the Prince of Wales crest and the regimental title. The officers, warrant officers and staff sergeants were distinguished by wearing a 'flash' or bow of black silk ribbon with long ends attached to the back of the tunic collar. This flash, in the eighteenth century, kept the tunic clean and prevented the heavily greased pigtail from spoiling it. The regiment, being abroad at the time the order was abolished when cut hair became fashionable, keep the flash to this day.

At the time of the print's publication, the regiment had served in India until 1896, and were then stationed in Aden. They returned home in 1897.

THE QUEEN'S ROYAL REGIMENT c. 1896

The Queen's Royal Regiment is the 2nd Regiment of Foot and was raised in 1661 as the Tangier Regiment. The nickname of the regiment was Kirkes Lambs, so called because of their Paschal lamb badge and because of their ferociousness under their Colonel Kirke.

From 1837 until 1880 the regimental march was a tune called 'The old Queens'. The national anthem was embodied into this march. In 1881 at a review at Aldershot before Queen Victoria and the Commander-in-Chief, the Duke of Cambridge, 'The old Queens' was played as the regiment marched past in review. Queen Victoria was not amused and enquired whether special permission had been given for the use of the national anthem saying, that unless it had, the practice must cease forthwith. No authority could be traced.

In 1883 Lieutenant-Colonel Kelly-Kelly, then commanding the 1st

The Queen's Royal Regiment c 1896

Battalion communicated through the Portuguese Ambassador with the King of Portugal. He mentioned the long association between the regiment and the ruling house of Braganza and explained the problem that had arisen and asked if a Portuguese march could be used by the regiment. Several were suggested and played by the 1st and 2nd battalions' bandmasters. Official approval however of the new regimental march 'Braganza' was not finally given until 1903 by the War Office.

Although the old march of the regiment 'The old Queens' could never again be played on parade after Aldershot Review of 1881, it was and still is the custom for the tune to be played immediately before the regimental march 'Braganza' on guest nights in the officers' mess.

The 2nd Battalion march is Scottish, 'We'll gang nae mair to yon toun'. This was due to the fact that the first colonel was Lieutenant-Colonel Bruce, late of the Highland Light Infantry. This battalion was raised at Colchester in Essex in August 1857.

The badge on the brass helmet plate depicts the pascal lamb, on a red background, on velvet for officers. Since 1911 a small scroll on the officers' helmets was inscribed 'The Queens'. The other ranks helmet plate has the garter inscribed 'West Surrey'.

KING'S OWN SHROPSHIRE LIGHT INFANTRY c. 1896

The regimental march of the 1st Battalion was that of the old 53rd (Shropshire) Regiment and called 'Old Towler'. That of the 2nd Battalion was 'The daughter of the regiment' which was also the march of the 85th (King's Light Infantry) Regiment. The two regiments were amalgamated in 1881 to form the King's Own Shropshire Light Infantry. The uniform was the same as that of the Line, except the cloth helmet was covered in a green cloth in place of blue, all the fittings were brass, and gilt for officers. The tunics were scarlet with royal blue facings.

The 1st Battalion had the nickname of 'The old Brickdusts', from the colour of the 53rd Regiment's facings. The 2nd Battalion had the nickname 'The elegant extracts', in allusion to the officers of the 85th Foot who were once selected from other regiments. Being a Light Infantry regiment, the marching pace was 140 to the minute. This dated back from the Peninsular War period when Light Infantry advanced rapidly as an independent force. Rifle regiments had the same pace. Other tunes were common to all regiments, an instance was the playing of 'The girl I left behind me' when the regiment left one station or barracks for another. It has been attributed to an Irish bandmaster of the eighteenth century who was able to fall in love with a girl at each place that the regiment was stationed, and he wrecked many a heart. When these young ladies came to see him off, tearfully, the band struck up this air, and the custom gradually spread throughout the army. Another march common to all regiments was the Rogues March, played when a soldier was discharged with ignominy and he was 'drummed out'. On reaching the barrack gates he was administered a final kick by the youngest drummer boy.

The sounding of Retreat on bugles every evening is another custom common to all British Infantry regiments, this is to give notice that the gates are to be shut in half an hour. In the eighteenth century soldiers were not allowed to take their arms out of their barracks or tents after the sounding of Retreat. Unless there is an alarm, this is the last call until the sounding of Reveille the next morning. Some regiments have adopted a different tune from the traditional Reveille to soften the rude awakening.

GRAND DUCHY OF HESSE-KASSEL: INFANTRY BAND 1830
This duchy had a much larger army than many of the other principalities at this date. The uniforms were copied from the Prussian and Russian

styles. The shako was of the bell-shaped pattern, made of black felt bound in leather at the top and bottom. The chin strap was of overlapping brass scales. Around the body of the headdress was a decoration of twisted white cord with a white tassel on the left; caplines passed down to the left shoulder strap and ended in two white cord tassels and flounders. At the front of the shako was a cockade in the national colours, a loop of white cord and a white metal button. The all-red plume denoted the Life Guard Regiment.

The prussian blue coatees were double-breasted with two rows of white metal buttons, eight in each row. The standing collar was of red cloth, edged with a white lace. The Guard's collar was further embellished with two bars of white lace with a showing of red light in between. The shoulder straps were white fastened by a white metal button, and were decorated with the Duke's monogram in brass. The bandsmen's wings were of red and white cloth with a white woollen fringe. The cuffs were of red cloth edged in white lace and ornamented with two bars of vertical white lace and a white metal button for the Guard Regiment. For the line the cuffs were slashed with white lace and three white metal buttons. The skirts of the coats' turnbacks were red, fastened with a white metal button. Over the right shoulder passed a buff leather belt to support a brass-hilted short infantry sword, carried in a black leather scabbard with brass mountings. White linen trousers were worn with white buttoned gaiters over black shoes.

The drummer also wore a white apron to protect his uniform. The drums were of brass with wooden hoops painted in the national colours of red and white.

The flute cases were carried on a narrow buff leather belt. The case was painted red.

The French horn depicted in this print was developed in the various German armies, and is a military musical instrument. A difficult instrument to play, it commanded a better wage for these particular bandsmen.

CENT GARDE TROMPETTE FRENCH 2nd EMPIRE 1860

In 1854 this regiment was formed to protect the Emperor and his immediate family, and to carry out duties in and around the palaces. The helmet was made of steel with a brass crest with a Medusa head at the front, above this a white tuft issued from a brass cup. From the top of the crest fell a white plume that reached halfway down the back of the guardsman. A triangular brass helmet plate depicted the crowned 'N' within a wreath of laurels. The plume was of red feathers, a red pom-pom at the base.

The tunic was scarlet with a standing collar, the front decorated with

Band of The 2nd Queen's Own Rifles of Canada 1898
Being a rifle regiment, the band consists of drums and bugles. In the centre
of the photograph stands Bugle Major Charles Swift, who had joined the
service at the age of eleven in 1866, becoming lead bugler and subsequently
Bugle Major.

The forty-five man band accompanied the regiment which took part in the
Louis Riel Campaign of 1885, acting in turn as duty buglers, musicians and
ambulance corps.
The uniform is dark green with scarlet facings, similar to the British King's
Royal Rifle Corps.

two bars of gold lace. The tunic was single-breasted and fastened by a row of brass buttons and seven bars of gold lace across the chest. The epaulettes had yellow straps with yellow and red mixed fringes. The sleeves were decorated with inverted chevrons of lace.

On mounted duties the skirts were buttoned back to reveal the blue lining. From the right shoulder was fastened a red and yellow twisted cord epaulette with brass ends. Over the left shoulder passed a white leather belt with brass fittings and a black leather pouch bearing a brass sunburst and the letter 'N'. Around the waist the belt was of white leather with a rectangular buckle of brass bearing the crowned 'N'.

The breeches were of white leather and fitted into tall black leather jack boots with steel spurs. White gauntlet gloves were worn.

2ᵉ EMPIRE
ESCADRON DES CENT GARDES

Cent Garde Trumpeter

Trooping the Colour

The shabraque was of scarlet cloth with a gold lace edge, the corners embroidered with the Imperial crown and cypher. The pistol holsters were comparisoned in a similar manner, but were not embroidered. The cloak which was carried behind the saddle was red and blue. The very tall cuirassiers sword had a brass hilt and was carried in a steel scabbard. The trumpets were silver bound with cords of gold and red. The trumpet banners were fringed in gold and edged in gold lace. The centre was embroidered with the complete coat of arms of the Bonapartes, on a field of red and blue. At the top left and right was embroidered gold sunbursts and the Imperial cypher. A scroll beneath the coat of arms depicted the regimental title.

TROOPING THE COLOUR SCOTS GUARDS BAND c. 1896

The Scots Guards band is seen passing the Grenadier Guards who are drawn up in review order for the Ceremony of Trooping the Colour. This ceremony is carried out by all British infantry regiments, but of course the most publicised is that of the Brigade of Guards. The Ceremony is carried out in rotation by Guards regiments on the Sovereign's birthday. Because the Sovereign is present, the drum major leading the band is in State dress. Each Guard arrives independently from the barracks led by band and drums, with the pipes as well, if the Scots or Irish Guards are present.

The massed bands are under the command of the senior drum major who gives all the commands. After inspecting the Guards, the band is then given the command to march in slow time towards the Colour at the far side of the parade ground. Four paces from the Colour, they countermarch and halt. They then move towards their original positions in quick time. As they do so, one drummer marches away to the right of the escort to the Colour. When the massed bands cease playing, the single drummer beats 'the drummers call'. This is the prelude to the handing over of the Colour to be trooped to the ensign. The drummer then rejoins the corps of drums. After the Colour has been trooped through the ranks, the band in the centre of the parade ground plays as the regiments march past the Sovereign, first in slow time and then at a quick pace. As the regiments reach the position by the Sovereign, the bands play the appropriate regimental march in slow or quick time. At the conclusion of the Parade, the massed bands lead the way to Buckingham Palace.

In the picture it may be noted that the officer is wearing the State dress red and gold sash and the gold laced sword belt.

On ordinary occasions the sash would be plain crimson and the sword belt white patent leather. Today the sash is worn around the waist with the sword belt underneath.

PIPERS

The pipes have been mentioned as a weapon of war by the unmusical, and the wail of the pipes has brought fear to many foes; it has not been proved if this was because of the pipes or the fierceness of the soldiery. It is certain, however, that these men have been spurred on to greater endeavours by the sound of the pipes

Scottish pipers are held in special affection by the people of Scotland, and the British Royal family are awakened, when in Scotland, by the playing of the pipes on the Castle walls, by the Queen's personal piper.

Pipers are all foot soldiers, however on the introduction of the pipes to the Indian army, they were adopted by the Bengal Lancers, the only regiment to play bagpipes on horseback. Thirty-eight Indian regiments adopted the pipes, although not all wore the tartan. In some regiments the tartan only covered the bag of the pipes and pipe ribbons.

In the European field the bagpipes are found in several countries. The earliest perhaps were known as the tibia utricularis of the Roman Legions, there were also the bignou pipes of Brittany, the calabrian and cornamusa of Italy and the sackpfeife of Germany. In France there was the musette and in the Low Countries the doodlesack.

Queen's Own Highlanders   Pipe Major John Allan   1st Battalion

Piper Arm Band   *Pipers Arm Badge*
MAJOR'S

Mention must also be made of the Irish pipes known as the Irish organs which have four drones. They were not as powerful as the Highland pipes. Special note has been made of the fact that the Highland pipes were referred to as an instrument of war. In the Highland Risings of 1715 and 1745, the Highlanders never marched without a piper, and therefore, in the eyes of the law the bagpipes were instruments of war, and as such were banned.

PIPES

The Scottish pipers have always been men of courage. A gallant incident occurred during the Tirah Campaign of 1897, the fighting was against the Afridis on the North West Frontier of India, and early in the attack on the practically impregnable heights at Dargai, Piper Findlater was shot in both legs, he sank to the ground, blood streaming from his most painful wounds, but continued playing Highland warlike tunes on his pipes. This gave great encouragement to his comrades as they crossed the bullet-swept ground. They tried to carry him to a place of safety so that his wounds could be attended to, but he refused help until the battle had been won. In recognition of his great courage he was awarded the Victoria Cross. A tune he played was called 'Cock o' the North' which has since then been adopted by his regiment, The Gordon Highlanders, as their

Scottish Piper

regimental march. The strains of pipes playing martial airs has always inspired the Scottish soldiers to even greater feats of courage. This fact is realised by the pipers themselves, who disregard all dangers in an effort to play tunes to cheer on their countrymen.

One of the earliest times that regimental pipes were played in battle was in India at Porto Novo in 1781. The British General, Sir Eyre Coote, promised a brave piper during the battle that he would present him with a set of silver pipes. He did not forget and the pipes were duly presented to the Battalion suitably inscribed. Another piper, George Clarke, during the battle of Vimiera on 28th August 1808, was wounded, but being set up by his comrades continued to play to his regiment, the Highland Light Infantry, in their advance against the French. Piper Kenneth Mackay of the 79th Queen's Own Cameron Highlanders was present at the battle of Waterloo and when the regiment had been formed into a square to await a charge of French cavalry, Mackay stepped out of the square and marched

Pipe Banner
The pipe major's banner usually has the battalion badge and battle honours worked on both sides. The Company banners usually have the battalion badge only on one side and the donor's crest on the reverse. It was quite common for the officers of the regiment to present these banners.

Pipers of the 17th Bengal Infantry 1901
This regiment was raised in 1858 and disbanded in 1921. Pipers were introduced to many Indian regiments by the Scots serving in the British army. It may be noted that the pipers are even wearing the Highland pattern doublets. The headquarters were at Benares and the men were drawn from Hindustani Mohammedans.

around the outside playing 'Cogadh no Sith' – 'Peace or War'. George III
heard of this incident and presented Piper Mackay with a set of silver
mounted bagpipes. When stationed in Paris after the battle, the Russian
Emperor asked to see and hear Piper Mackay, who played 'Cogadh no
Sith'.

At the battle of Loos in 1915 during the First World War, Piper Daniel
Laidlaw of the King's Own Scottish Borderers continued with the tradi-
tions of playing the pipes in even the worst conditions. As the Battalion was
about to attack, the Germans filled their trenches with gas, as the Scots
coughed and choked they could hear their regimental march 'Blue Bonnets
over the Border' being played by Piper Laidlaw as he marched along the
parapet of the trenches, heedless of bullets or gas. The men threw themselves over the top and attacked the German lines. Daniel Laidlaw was
awarded the Victoria Cross. In the Canadian army there are many
Highland regiments who emulate the customs of their common ancestors
in Scotland. The Canadian pipers are also just as resolute. Piper
James Richardson of the Manitoba Regiment was only eighteen when the
regiment was fighting in the Somme during 1916. When attacking the
Germans the regiment was held up by a barbed wire entanglement. Men
died and the regiment was suffering with heavy casualties, it became a
demoralising situation. Piper Richardson realised this and at once
marched up and down the wire playing his pipes with great coolness. The
desired effect was accomplished, the wire was broken and the regiment
won its objective. After helping wounded soldiers back to their trenches,
he returned to the wire for his pipes and was killed. He was also awarded
the Victoria Cross.

Some of the Highland pipers were very young. In the Argyll and
Sutherland Highlanders it was a piper of fourteen who, playing 'The
Haughs of Crondel', squeezed through the hole blasted in the Sikander-
bargh during the Indian Mutiny of 1857. He was killed, fighting fiercely
hand to hand. The battle was eventually won.

An even younger piper of twelve years old played 'Cock o' the North' at
Shah Najaf, provoking a fusillade of bullets from the defending Sepoy
troops. He, however, survived.

In the United States of America pipes were introduced by the Scots
settlers. There were pipers with the Militia of the West Virginia countries
in the war of 1775 and there is mention of a piper playing on the walls of
The Alamo on the day before the last Mexican assault. This was John
McGregor who with Davy Crockett used to conduct musical duets for the
amusement of the defenders of The Alamo Mission in 1836.

In the American Civil War of 1861, the 79th New York State Militia were raised from men of Scottish birth, they soon discarded their kilts, but were recorded wearing Cameron tartan trews at the first battle of the war, Bull Run, in 1861, and on parades were led by their regimental pipers. Today the pipers of Scotland are to be found in the United States Air Force Band formed in 1965. The original uniforms were made in Scotland and delivered to the band in 1960 while they were on tour in England. The tartan chosen was the Mitchell plaid to honour General Billy Mitchell, the great champion of the United States Air Force. The Highland doublet is of dark blue cloth, faced in white; for evening wear pipers have a sporran of seal skin. The hose are of Mitchell tartan with scarlet ribbon garters. The headdress for pipers is the glengarry of dark blue with a red toorie and black ribbons. The drum major wears a highland feather bonnet with a white cut feather plume on the left hand side.

In the old Indian army of the British Raj many pipers were included in the forces. The Gurkha regiments were especially fond of them. In the Indian army the 40th Bengal Infantry (Pathans) had pipers but did not wear a tartan, instead they wore Kohat Turghis which were draped over the shoulder as a plaid and were held by a regimental crest on the shoulder

Teaching the Bagpipes 1898
The Highland Piper in this photograph is the Pipe Major of the Queen's Own Cameron Highlanders. His pupils are from the 2nd and 9th Sudanese Battalions of the Egyptian Army. The 9th were brigaded with the Queen's Own Cameron Highlanders in the 1884–5 Campaign on the Nile and were nicknamed the 2nd Battalion Cameron Highlanders.

itself. The tunics were drab with piping and shoulder straps of green. The headdress was a drab pagri with a green kullah.

Another Indian regiment with pipers, this time with Campbell plaid tartans, was the 38th Dogras, their sister regiment, the 37th Dogras, had pipers carrying the MacKenzie tartan on the bagpipes and ribbons.

The Royal Garhwal Rifles were equipped with pipers in the Black Watch (42nd Highlanders) tartan, they wore silver lace chevrons on rifle green cloth tunics. This regiment was later incorporated in the Independent Indian Army.

Between the two World Wars a pipe band was maintained by the Royal Bombay Sappers and Miners. They did not wear tartan, but wore the usual red tunics faced with royal blue, the collar piped white and the pointed cuffs with white cord austrian knots. Dark blue knickerbockers with a red stripe and dark blue puttees were worn. The pipe banner was of blue cloth with a gold fringe and was embroidered with regimental devices.

Scottish Pipers

Today the pipers have not disappeared from the Indian Continent. The Pakistan Artillery have a band of pipers and the Indian Punjab Regiment also have pipers. Both wear the plaids but not kilts. Further east, the Hong Kong Police have a pipe band. This regiment wears white tunics and blue trousers with spats. They wear a highland bonnet and the pipers carry a blue banner bearing the Police crest in silver embroidery. The Kingdom of Jordan, having received for many years British military advisors and equipment has also introduced Highland pipers. These men wear the usual army khaki uniform with white equipment for parades and the pipers are without banners although they do carry ribbons. Another Arab state, that of Libya, had in the days of King Idris before the revolution, a pipe band, formed from the police. The pipers wore the usual dress of a white tunic with blue trousers. The pipes were without banners but carried ribbons in the national colours of green, black and red.

1st BATTALION SCOTS GUARDS c. 1870
In 1856 a pipe major and five pipers were officially allowed for each battalion; previously pipers had been attached to the companies at the officers' personal expense. Now they were to receive one shilling and two pence daily plus one penny beer money.

This photograph shows, in the centre of the group, the first pipe major of the 1st Battalion Scots Guards, sergeant Ewan Henderson. He had accompanied the battalion to the Crimea War. His rank is shown by the four silver chevrons and crown above the cuffs. The unofficial tartan trews he is wearing were made from old kilts. The pipe major holds a personal warrant in the Household pipers and frequently plays at the Royal Palaces. The pipers also play round the table of the officers' mess after dinner, and the pipe major afterwards drinks a loyal toast in Gaelic: '*Deoch slainte na ban righ*' which means 'Here's a health to the Woman King'.

Each company of the battalion has its own pipe march and, if detached from the battalion, its own piper.

The regimental march is 'Heilan' Laddie', a march of ancient origins dating back to at least 1692. The slow march is 'The Garb of old Gaul', composed in 1772.

The drum major, leaning against the wall, is wearing the undress cap with diced border and gold gimp-edged peak; there was a line of gold russia braid around the welt. The red tunic is laced in gold. The collar is low with a rounded front, embroidered with a thistle badge on each side, in silver wire. The slashed cuffs are dark blue with gold. The bandsmen's wings also bear the regimental crest: 'The Order of the Thistle'. The sash over the right shoulder is crimson, the trousers blue, with a broad red stripe. The sword belt is of white leather with a brass buckle. The sword has a brass hilt, the guard bearing the regimental badge. The scabbard is of black leather with brass mountings.

This photograph was taken at Wellington Barracks, Windsor.

PRINCESS LOUISE'S ARGYLL AND SUTHERLAND HIGH-LANDERS c. 1896

The pipers' dress has changed little since the middle of the last century. The glengarry is worn today by the whole regiment. Previously all ranks, including the pipers, had worn the Kilmarnock bonnet, but this was replaced by the glengarry in the 1850s.

The green doublet was single-breasted with a standing collar of the same colour. The buttons were of brass. The gauntlet cuffs were ornamented with three brass buttons and white cord. The Inverness flaps had the same decoration as the cuffs, edged with two rows of white cord. The pipers wore bandsmen's wings and these were piped gold. The waistbelt was of black leather with a white metal buckle. The crossbelt was also of black leather with white metal mountings. The collar badges and the badge on the buckle was the crest of the regiment and was designed by their Colonel-in-Chief, the Princess Louise; it combined the Argyll boar's head and the Sutherland wild cat within two wreaths, surmounted by the princess's own monogram and coronet. Below was the regimental motto, NE OBLIVISCARIS.

The kilt was the Sutherland tartan. The tartan hose were held by red garters and worn with white buttoned gaiters over the shoes. A plaid was worn on the left shoulder fixed by a plaid brooch of regimental pattern. The sporran was of white goat hair and decorated with three black tails, the top of the sporran being embellished with the regimental badges. On his right side the officer ~~piper~~ wore a dirk of special pattern. The pipers wore a dirk made with white metal mounts instead of the officer's silver,

Argyll and Sutherland Highlanders

and a plain blade in place of that engraved with the regimental crest and battle honours.

The piper was unarmed except for this weapon, but would of course be busy playing the pipes in times of battle at the forefront of the advancing regiment, a tradition that has not been broken to this day.

The pipes were decorated with a pipe banner bearing the regimental crest on one side and the donor's crest on the other. It was the custom for well-born officers to buy pipe banners and so have their own crest on the opposite side to the regimental crest.

Gordon Highlanders 1896

THE GORDON HIGHLANDERS c. 1896

The piper of the Gordon Highlanders wore the glengarry: the only pipers to wear the feather bonnets at this period were the Black Watch. The badge depicted the stag's head within a wreath of ivy with a scroll below: BYDAND, meaning 'stand fast'. The stag's head was the crest of the Marquis of Huntly, and the ivy wreath, the badge of the Gordon family.

The tartan worn by the piper – and the regiment – was an unusual pattern with a yellow overstripe. The highest rank of the pipers was pipe major, the equivalent of a drum major. Before a piper could qualify for this rank he had to be able to compose music as well as play marches, strathspeys and pibrochs. In barracks the piper regulated the Highlander's day, rousing him in the morning with one tune, and calling him to lunch or dinner with another. The duty piper warned the officers of the time to dress for mess and provided music for dinner, and on guest nights the pipe major and several other pipers were present and audible.

The pipes consist of four pipes, a blow-pipe and a leather bag, seasoned to make it water-tight. Three of the pipes are drones, with sliding joints for tuning, the sound itself coming from cane reeds inserted in their lower sections. These three drones are tuned to a chord to harmonise with the melody pipe or chanter, which the piper fingers with both hands.

The piper of the Gordon Highlanders had a green doublet with brass buttons and the regimental goat-hair sporran decorated with two tails. The plaid on the right shoulder was held by a plaid brooch in the regimental pattern. The red and black diced hose were held by red garters, and white spats covered the shoes.

The royal tiger collar badges were awarded after nineteen strenuous years fighting in India. These were first awarded in 1806.

Until 1932 the regimental march was 'Highland Laddie', shared with the Scots Guards. After that date the march of the Gordon Highlanders became 'Cock o' the North'.

72nd REGIMENT

The 72nd Regiment were raised in 1778 as the 78th Highlanders, renumbered the 72nd in 1786. The first commander was the Earl of Seaforth. The regiment lost its Highland identity in 1809, but this was restored in 1823.

The piper wears the uniform which was worn in India where the regiment was serving, in the 1790s, under the command of Lord Cornwallis; in the campaigns against Tippoo Sahib, at the siege of Pondicherry and the reduction of the island of Ceylon. In 1798 the battalion returned home to Scotland to raise new recruits, and was based at Perth.

72nd Highlanders

The pipers were not strictly part of the band, but were members of the fighting regiment. Consequently they wore uniforms similar to those of the rank and file. For service in India they had a blue bonnet with a red tuft on top, the diced border being of red and white with a green tape running through. A black leather sweatband ran around the bottom edge. Their coat was of red cloth, the stand and fall collar of yellow cloth with a regimental button and a bastion-ended white lace decoration on each side of the open collar. The yellow lapels were buttoned back with white metal buttons, each button hole decorated with bastion-ended white lace. Shoulder straps were yellow, edged in white lace, and ending in white worsted tufts. The cuffs were also yellow with three white metal buttons and bastion-ended lace. The turnbacks were white and fitted with a regimental device. On each side of the back were pocket flaps with buttons and button loops.

The waistcoat was buff or off-white and fastened by a row of white metal buttons. The buff leather belt worn over the right shoulder carried the Highland sword. The belt was fastened by a belt plate made of brass in the form of an oval, stamped with the royal crown and the number 72. The Highland sword had a steel basket hilt lined with red cloth and decorated with a red fringe. The blade was plain. It was carried in a black leather scabbard with steel fittings.

Trousers for wear in India were of white linen and were worn with the normal Highland shoes or pumps with steel buckles. The bagpipes are shown with red and yellow cord tassel decorations and the bag of the pipes green.

Pipers are trained soldiers and though the brass band may remain behind in time of war, the pipers always accompany the battalion into action. Also, the duty piper sounds all calls in Highland regiments, from parade to lights out.

BLACK WATCH c. 1896

Independent companies of Highlanders were formed in 1739 into a complete regiment. In 1751 they were numbered the 42nd Regiment. In 1881 the 73rd Foot was made the 2nd Battalion of the Black Watch. The 73rd had been raised in 1787 as the 2nd Battalion of the Black Watch and so returned to the parent regiment in the amalgamations of 1881. In 1758 the facings were changed to royal blue, having previously been buff. The name 'Black Watch' is derived from the dark tartan worn by independent companies, this is a simple sett of black, blue and green, without over-stripes. It was not connected with any Highland clan and was called the Government tartan.

The piper wore the Royal Stewart tartan. The doublet was dark green, similar to those worn by other Highland regimental pipers. The feather bonnet carried on the left side a red hackle, only worn by the Black Watch since 1882, other regiments were forbidden to wear it after that date. The pipe ribbons and bag were also in the Royal Stewart tartan. The march of

The Black Watch

the regiment was 'Highland Laddie', known by regimental custom as 'Heilan Laddie'.

The piper wore the Highland sword which he would take up in action and drop the pipes; later only the dirk was worn. At a later date the piper played all through the action; various tunes were used, triumphant or rarely, in retreat.

Drummers wore the regimental uniform with drummers' wings on the shoulders, the band lace was sewn on the piping of the doublet.

Drummers did not usually wear a sporran because of the drum. If it was worn, the sporran was carried at one side. The spats worn by pipers and drummers were introduced for guard duties in 1826 and made of white drill with square fronts, a traditional Black Watch feature.

The badge was the Order of the Thistle, it consisted of a wreath of thistles. Within the wreath was an oval inscribed 'Nemo me impune lacessit', and within the oval was St. Andrew and the cross. Above the oval was a crown, and below, the sphinx. Two separate scrolls were inscribed 'Royal Highlanders' and 'Black Watch'.

Band of the Nizam of Hyderabad 1903
This photograph shows one of the bands in the entourage of the Nizam of Hyderabad at the Delhi Durbar to celebrate the coronation of the King, Emperor of India, Edward VII.
All the instruments appear to be European The most interesting feature of course is the fact that the entire band was made up of ladies.

Hyderabad Military Band 1903
This photograph illustrates a group
of infantry bandsmen from the army
of the Nizam of Hyderabad, the
most powerful of the Indian princes,
with an army at that time of
approximately 37,000 foot and
8,000 cavalry. The man in the
dark uniform is titled bandmaster,
although he is carrying a brass
instrument. The group at the front
are all bugle boys.

SCRAPBOOK OF BANDS AND UNIFORMS

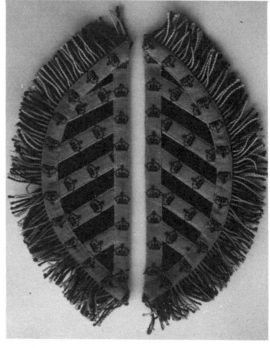

Drummer Arm Emblem   *Bandsmen Epaulettes*
MAJOR

The Grand Duchy of Mecklenburg-Schwerin Grenadier Guard Regiment

Oldenburg Band

West Point Band, 1818

Band of the 9th Dragoons 1897
The band of the French 9th Dragoons are standing in the courtyard of the Cavalry Barracks at Lunéville in Lorraine, one of the great cavalry stations that were within a day's ride of the German frontier. The Barracks were built in 1702 as a Palace by Leopold, Duke of Lorraine.

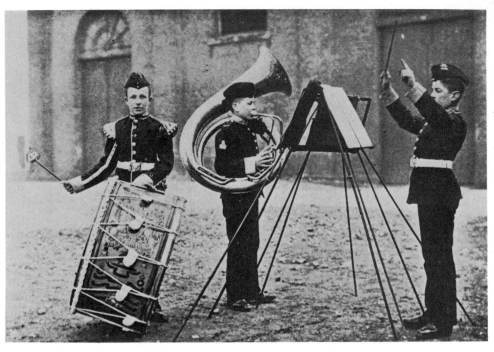

The Royal East Kent Regiment   1899
The band boys practising at the barracks in Brighton where the 2nd Battalion was then
stationed. The boy on the left is wearing the full dress band tunic with a foreign cap.
Note the band lyre on the boy's sleeve in the centre.

Band of the Hyderabad Lancers of the Golconda Brigade   1896
The Army of the Nizam of Hyderabad included two brigades of picked troops, "The
Golconda Brigade" and the "Reformed Troops". Two regiments of Lancers were formed
in 1892, these bandsmen belonging to those Regiments. The Bandmaster is on the left and
the kettledrums may be seen in the centre. The banners are apparently plain.

SLG

TRUMPETER

Metropolitan Garrison Artillery Australia 1898
The drum major and (bugler) belonged to the Australian Militia Artillery that were formed to protect the extensive coastline of Australia in the nineteenth century.
The drum major's uniform has some interesting features: the white pith helmet has a large grenade badge, his bandsmen's wings appear to have quite a long fringe to them, and the drum major's staff has a very large grenade as the head, made in brass or white metal.

*Brazilian
Drummer*

*Brazilian
Trumpeter*

Brazilian Flute

French Footguards 1900

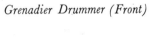

Grenadier Drummer (Front)

Grenadier Drummer (Back)

Drum Major   Grenadier Guards   c.1900
The drum major wears the scarlet tunic with gold lace on the front and sleeves. His badge of rank, hardly discernible, consists of four bar chevrons, points upwards, above the right cuff. The drum major's sash is of blue cloth heavily embroidered in gold and silver, bearing the regimental crest and battle honours. The medals he is wearing are for services in the Sudan campaigns.

Drum Major State Dress

State Drummer

State Dress 1st Life Guards Bandsmen

HELMETS THE ROYAL BERKSHIRE REGIMENT THE MIDDLE-
SEX REGIMENT (DUKE OF CAMBRIDGE'S OWN)

These two blue cloth helmets are the types worn by the band from 1878
to 1914, and then sporadically by the corps of drums up to the
present day. This helmet was greatly influenced by the German pickelhaube, the German Empire having just won the Franco-Prussian War.
French style shakos were redundant.

In 1878, order No. 40 of the 1st May decreed that this was to be the
Home Service helmet. It was made of cork and covered with blue cloth,
dark green for rifle and light infantry regiments. The peak was rounded
and not bound in gilt metal as for officers, although some drum majors
are seen today wearing an officer's pattern helmet. At the top was a brass
cross piece and a spike, ball top for Royal Artillery and certain other corps.
A chin chain of brass mounted on leather issued from a rose fitting on the
left side. It could be hooked to the rose fitting on the right or on the hook at
the back of the cross piece on the top of the helmet. The universal brass
eight-pointed star with a crown at the top, carried in the centre the
regimental badge, this could be removed and used as a pagri badge on the
Indian service helmet.

Royal Berkshire Helmet

Middlesex Regiment Helmet

Royal regiments have scarlet cloth backings to the centre badge. In the officer's helmet this is of scarlet velvet.

The Royal Berkshire Regiment shows the stag under the tree, the badge of the Berkshire Militia, alluding to the great Royal Forest at Windsor. The Middlesex Regiment plate shows within a wreath of laurels, the crest of the Prince of Wales with below, the coronet and monogram of the Duke of Cambridge resting on the battle honour 'Albuhera'. This was fought in 1811 during the Peninsular campaign, and resulted in the loss of 400 men and 22 officers killed and wounded, out of a total of 570, all ranks. Their stubborn valour acquired them the nickname 'The Diehards'. For Volunteer and Militia regiments the helmet fittings were of white metal or in silver for officers.

These helmets were supplied before the First World War at two pounds ten shillings, for the officer's pattern, unfortunately no record for the price of other ranks has been kept.

BAND HELMET ROYAL ARTILLERY 1879

In 1878 it was decided to replace the bandsmen's sable busby with a helmet. In the same year the regiment had adopted the blue cloth Germanic helmet in line with all the other British infantry regiments. The band helmet differed from that issued to the rest of the regiment in having a rounded peak bound in brass. The binding continued all the way round the helmet. This was in fact taken from the regular cavalry helmet of that time. The helmet plate was of the officer's pattern, the complete royal coat of arms with the regimental badge below, and a scroll with 'ubique' with the cannon, the whole resting on a scroll reading 'Quo fas et gloria ducant'. Officer's pattern rosettes at the sides held the gilt link chain chin strap on a blue velvet lining. On the top of the helmet was the standard pattern cross piece with a laurel leaf cup holding a ball. From the top of the ball issued a falling red horse hair plume reaching down the back peak. In 1895 the band re-adopted the busby, although the regiment retained the blue cloth helmet.

Royal Artillery Helmet   *Royal Artillery Bandmaster's Busby*

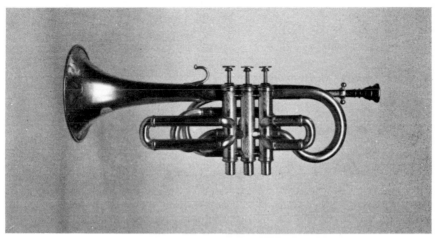

Keyed Bugle

RECORDS OF MILITARY BAND MUSIC

The Band of the Irish army Studio Two TWO 375
Tanks in concert PRI 1st Royal Tank Regiment
The Gay and gallant (Gordon Highlanders) Waverley SZLP 2310
The 1967 Edinburgh military tattoo Waverley SZLP 2095
The piper's parade Waverley SZLP 2092
Cock o' the north Waverley SZLP 2069
Marching with the Royal Scots Waverley SZLP 2072
The 1966 Edinburgh military tattoo Waverley SZLP 2080
In concert – The Life Guards CBS 64877
Bands and drums Royal Welch Fusiliers SNP 223
Music of the Light Division RT 1329
In London with the Coldstream Guards Eclipse ECS 2101
Marching with the Marines SRS 5112
Band of the RAF Regiment Invicta INV 101
Band of the Royal Marines Portsmouth Philips 6308048
Band of the Scots Guards Philips 630068
Military musical pageant Philips 6308078
Salute to Karl King – The Life Guards Philips SBL 7925
Band of the Royal Engineers Redifusion Z583
Band spectacular – Grenadier Guards Decca SKL 5096
Tattoo in Berlin Decca SKL 5042
British tournament and tattoo Decca SKL 5020
The world of military bands 2 Vols Decca SPA 66
Highlights from a military musical pageant Decca PFS 4186
March in Review – Grenadier Guards Decca PFS 4171
Massed band spectacular 6 Vols Drum Major MCN 6

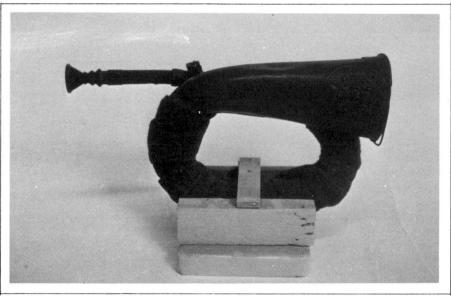

Russian Bugle

2nd Battn. – The Royal Anglian Regt. Drum Major MCN 2
Colchester tattoo Drum Major VP 283
Pipes and drums – Queen's Own Cameron Highlanders Beltona SBE 120
Marches of the vanishing regiments BBC Records REB 895
Band of the Welsh Guards BBC Records REC 1215
Band of the Durham Light Infantry Jackson JRC-S 5120
Scotland forever – The Royal Scots Greys International 1110
The changing of the Guard Fabri and Partners TGM X2
Sounds ceremonial – The Black Watch Pye NSPL 18341
Marching en route – The Black Watch Columbia TWO 333
The Gordons for you – The Gordon Highlanders Columbia SCX 6409
March of the Royal Highlanders Columbia TWO 292
The Brigade of Ghurkas Columbia Studio 2 TWO 342
Sousa marches – Royal Academy Sandhurst Music for Pleasure MFP 2147
Men of Harlech – The Welsh Guards Marble Arch 1320
The soldiers of the Queen – Chelsea Pensioners Marble Arch MSLS 1283
Pipes and drums 8th Batt. Royal Scots Marble Arch MAL 1132
Great marches – the Royal Artillery Allegro ALL 833
The Liverpool Scottish Allegro ALL 829
A life on the ocean wave – Royal Marines Hallmark HM 525
The Queen's Royal Irish Hussars Hallmark HM 617
Follow the guns with the Royal Artillery Golden Guinea GSGL 10446
Second to none Golden Guinea GSGL1
Sousa plays Sousa and other cylinders Golden Guinea GGL L431
1812 – Band of the Scots Guard Fontana LPS 16264
Pipes and drums – Queen's Own Highlanders Great Bands Records GBS 1001

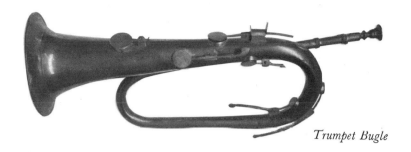

Trumpet Bugle

Band of the Royal Engineers Sagra Eros 8128
The sound of Her Majesty's Royal Marines Liberty LST 7429
Trooping the Colour London SP 44044
The pipes and drums of Ireland London SW 99232
Pomp and ceremony London SW 99352
The Black Watch – War pipe and plaid London SW 99407
Pomp and circumstance London PS 317
The Queen's birthday salute Vanguard VSD 2011
Pipes and drums of the 1st Battalion Scots Guards Fiesta FLPS 1490
Marschmusik Fiesta FLP 1367
Militaermusik aus vier Jahrhunderten Fiesta FLP 1420
Blue bonnets over the Border Odeon PCS 3015
Greek marches Odeon
Parada militar Odeon LCLP 181
Marchas militares Espanolas Odeon LCLP 120
Die Schoensten Maersche aus Oesterreich Odeon 73530
Military fanfares, marches and choruses from the time of Napoleon Nonsuch H 71075
Marches de la 1ere division Francaise Libre Festival FLDZ 364
La fanfara dei Bersaglieri RCA Ital. PML 100455
Favorite marches RCA Camden CAS 474
The U.S. Army band and chorus RCA Victor LSP 2685
The U.S. Navy band and the sea chanters RCA Victor LSP 2688

Key Bugle

Bass Tuba

The U.S. Marine band RCA Victor LSP 2687
The U.S. Air Force band and the singing sergeants RCA Victor LSP 2686
Marschmusik am Brandenburg-Preussischen Hofe 1685–1823 Telefunken SIT 43
    104-B
Reiterfreunden Vol 1 Polydor SLPHM 237 064
Reiterfreunden Vol 2 Polydor SLPHM 237 434
Der grosse Zapfenstreich Telefunken SLE 14 210
Was alte Camaraden singen Volksplatte SNVP 6093
Es war ein Edelweiss Golden 12 LP 107
The Royal Ulster Rifles Available from The Royal Irish Rangers, Belfast
On the square – Royal Marines School of Music HMV & CSD 3703
Scottish pipe favourites – The Black Watch Columbia TWO 344
Band of the Sherwood Foresters Available from the regiment
Marching with the Tigers – Royal Leicester Rgt. Available from the regiment
Pipes and drums – 10th Princess Mary's Ghurka Rifles Ghurka Welfare Appeal
Trumpet calls and bugle calls – Royal Artillery Available from the regiment
Fanfare du 13ieme Bataillon de Chasseure Alpins Philips 842.175
Musique des equipages de la Flotte Philips 842.177·
Musique et chantes des parachutistes Philips 842.197

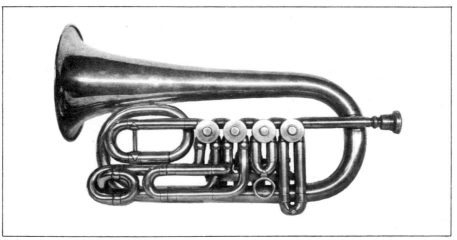

Trumpet

Mounted Drum

BIBLIOGRAPHY

Die Oesterreichische Armee 1700–1867 Vienna 1895

Uniformenkunde 18 vols Knötel 1890–1921

Handbuch der Uniformenkunde Knötel 1937

Der bunte Rock P. Martin SPRING BOOKS 1963

Vom Brustharnisch zum Waffenrock H. Schneider HUBER & CO. 1968

Die Preussische Armee unter Friederich Wilhelm II und Friederich Wilhelm III 1786– 1907 P. Martin KELLER & CO. 1963

Die Preussische Armee 1840–71 P. Martin KELLER & CO. 1970

Die Preussische Armee 1808–39 P. Martin KELLER & CO. 1972

Die Französische Armee 1789–1807 P. Martin KELLER & CO. 1969

Formations und uniformierunggeschischte des Preussischen Heeres 1808–1914 2 vols Paul Pietch SCHULZ 1966

Hertzogin Viktoria Luis hertzogin Viktoria Luis GOTTINGER VERLAGSANSTALT 1969

Deutchlands Ruhmeshalle. H. Muller-Bohn 1937

L'Armée Russe sous le Tsar Alexander I Paris 1955

Dix siècles de costume militaire HACHETTE 1965

Histoire Universelle des armées 4 vols Paris 1966

Les uniforms de l'armée francais terre, mer, air M. Toussaint & E. Bucquoy 1935

Les Suisses au service étranger J. Bory NYON & CIE 1965

L'armée Russe 1854, Lt-Colonel Pajol Paris 1854

Les vrais soldats de Napoléon L. Quennevat SEQUOIA-ELSEVIER 1968

Atlas de la Grand Armée L. Quennevat SEQUOIA-ELSEVIER 1966

L'armée Francais, ses uniformes, son armament, son equipment Current series of plates Paris

L'armée Russe 3 vols W. Zueguintzow PRIVATELY 1969

Drummer Grenadier of Imperial Guard

Drummer Imperial Guard

THE DRUM MAJOR,
OF THE ROYAL ARTILLERY.

A Lomax, 1st Dragoon Guards.

Lloyd Lith. to Her Majesty.

Uniformes des regiments francais de Louis XV à nos jours Paris 1945
Les regiments sous Louis XV Paris 1882
Album du guide des uniformes de l'armée francais 1780–1848 H. Malibran Paris 1907
Histoire de l'armeé francais 1872–1914 8 vols Galot & Robert
Album militaire BOUSSARD VALADON & CIE Paris 1890
Le uniformi piu belle del mondo oggi 2 vols R.D'Ami AMZ 1966
L'uniforme Italiana A. Gasparinetti EDIZIONI UNIVERALI 1965
Cronica del Trafe militar en Mexico del Siglo XVI al XX J. Hefter 1955
Uniformi militari Italiane 2 vols V. Delguidice BRAMANTS 1968
Zolnierz Polski B. Gembarzewski 4 vols Warsaw 1964
De Nederlandse cavalerie P. Forbes Wels C. VAN DISHOECK 1963
De Nederlandse infanterie H. Ringoir C. VAN DISHOECK 1968
British Military Uniforms from contemporary sources W. Y. Carman HILL 1957
Indian Army Uniforms 2 vols W. Y. Carman HILL MORGAN-GRAMPIAN 1961
The Russian Army under Nicholas I 1825–55 N. C. Durham 1965
A history of the British Army Fortesque London 1911
Military drawings and paintings in the collection of Her Majesty the Queen 2 vols
        PHAIDON 1966–70
India's army D. Jackson SAMPSON LOW 1940
Armies of India Lovett and McMunn A & C BLACK 1911
Durbar M. Merpes A & C BLACK 1903
Military Uniforms in colour Kannick BLANDFORD PRESS 1961
Cavalry uniforms Wilkinson-Latham & Cassin-Scott BLANDFORD PRESS 1969
Infantry uniforms Wilkinson-Latham & Cassin-Scott 2 vols BLANDFORD PRESS
        1970

The Green Howards' Drum Major

Silver Side Drum

One of a set of silver side drums made for the North
Staffordshire Regiment. All the designs, crests and
battle honours are raised up from the actual shell in
repoussé. In the late 1930's these cost about £30 each.

Drum Major's Staff Head   Rampur State India   c. 1920

This drum major's staff head depicts the coat of arms of the Maharajah of Rampur and
was made for one of his infantry regiment bands. The top is decorated with a crescent and
star. The head is made in silver with raised crest and lettering, hall marked. The cane is
ebony with sterling silver chains and a long ferrule. At this period the cost for this staff
was £40.

The anatomy of glory H. Brown LUND HUMPHRIES 1961
History of the uniforms of the British army 5 vols London 1940–67
The armies of Europe Major General G. McClellan 1861
British military uniforms Laver PENGUIN 1948
The Queen's Guards H. Legg Bourke MACDONALD 1965
Great Regiments V. Melegari WEIDENFELD AND NICHOLSON 1969
Battle Dress F. Wilkinson GUINNESS 1970
The army in India 1850–1914 Hutchinson N.A. MUSEUM 1968
German army uniforms and insignia 1933–45 B. Davis ARMS & ARMOUR PRESS 1971
German military uniforms and insignia 1933–45 W.E. INC. 1967
Types of the Indian army F. Bremner BELL OF ARMS LTD 1964
Illustrated histories of the Scottish regiments 3 vols P. Groves & H. Payne JOHNSTON
    LTD 1893
Pictorial history of the United States army G. Gurney CROWN 1966
The armies of today Brigadier General Merritt 1893
French army regiments and uniforms W. Thornburn ARMS & ARMOUR PRESS 1969

French Revolution Drum Major Front

*French Revolution
Drum Major Back*

The French Army 1914

Soldiers of the American army F. P. Todd New York 1941

Historical description of the uniforms and armaments of the Russian army 30 vols St Petersburg 1844–56

Military fashion J. Mollo BARRIE & JENKINS 1972

German army, navy uniforms and insignia 1871–1918 E. Hoffschmidt & W. Tantum W.E. INC. 1968

The age of Napoleon M. Davidson & J. Herold HORIZON 1963

History of the regiments of the British army Major R. Barnes SEELEY SERVICE 1950

The British army of 1914 Major R. Barnes SEELEY SERVICE 1968

The soldiers of London Major R. Barnes SEELEY SERVICE 1963

Military uniforms of Britain and the Empire Major R. Barnes SEELEY SERVICE 1960

Dictionary of music and musicians Grove MACMILLAN

Oxford companion of music Scholes OXFORD UNIVERSITY PRESS

Pelican book of musical instruments Baines PENGUIN BOOKS

Treatise on the military band H. Adkins BOOSEY AND HAWKES

Woodwind instruments and their history A. Baines FABER

The rise of military music H. Farmer W. REEVES 1912

History of the Royal Artillery Band H. Farmer R.A. INSTITUTION 1954

Handels kettledrums and other papers on military music H. Farmer

La musique militaire Michael Brenet Paris 1917

A hundred years of military music, the story of Kneller Hall P. Binns BLACKMORE PRESS

The story of the bagpipe W. H. Gratton SCOTT

European and American musical instruments A. Baines FABER

The brass band movement J. F. Russel and J. Elliott DENT

The uniforms and history of the Scottish regiments Major R. Barnes SEELEY SERVICE 1960

Uniforms of the United States army 2 vols H. Ogden 1907

The ancient art of warfare 2 vols J. Boudet BARRIE & ROCKLIFF 1966

Trumpet Cords

INDEX

Drum Major's Tunic

Scottish Piper

Drum Major (Back)

Key Bugle

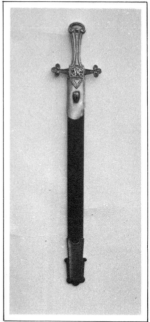

Band Sword

ACKNOWLEDGEMENTS

The authors gratefully acknowledge all those who have helped in the preparation of this book. These include David Leech of Potters Drums Ltd., Aldershot, Sterling Publishing Co. Inc. (U.S.A.) Captain R. Hollies-Smith and the Parker Gallery, London, The reference library of A. R. Fabb Bros. Ltd., Maidenhead, Berks, Boosey and Hawkes Museum, Edgware, Middlesex, Major R. G. Bartelot of the Royal Artillery Institution, Woolwich, London, W. A. Mann, Cassin Studios, London, The Soldier Magazine, Col. J. Martel, Musee de l'Armee, Paris, and Boris Mollo, National Army Museum, London. Special photography by Jack Blake of London.
Potters Drums Ltd. (*13, 17, 18, 19, 30, 42, 43, 49, 52, 65, 66, 112*), Sterling Publishing Co. Inc. (*45, 128* lower), Parker Gallery (*94, 95, 98, 99, 101, 102, 107, 116, 119, 120, 124, 131*), A. R. Fabb Bros. (*12, 27, 28, 31, 32, 33, 36, 37, 41, 44, 50, 51, 53, 57, 58, 59, 61, 62, 67, 68, 69, 70, 71, 72, 74, 75, 77, 79, 80, 81, 86, 87, 91, 93, 96, 103, 105, 106, 109, 113, 115, 117, 125, 126, 128* upper, *129, 130, 135, 136, 137, 149*), John Fabb (*138, 139, 140*). Boosey and Hawkes Museum (*16, 20, 21, 22, 23, 24, 26, 29, 141, 143, 144, 156*), Royal Artillery Institution (*34, 39, 40, 55, 63, 82, 84, 89, 90, 92, 134, 142, 145, 147, 152, 153*). W. A. Mann (*122*), Cassin Studios (*25, 46, 54, 78, 127, 132*). Soldier Magazine (*110, 111, 148, 154*). Musee de l'Armee Paris (*10, 11, 14, 15, 73, 133, 146, 150, 151, 155*), National Army Museum (*83*).